THE END OF WORK AS YOU KNOW IT

D1516236

8 STRATEGIES TO REDEFINE WORK ON YOUR OWN TERMS

MILO SINDELL AND **THUY SINDELL, PhD**

TEN SPEED PRESS
Berkeley

Ten Speed Press and the Ten Speed Press colophon are registered
trademarks of Random House, Inc.

Library of Congress Cataloging-in-Publication Data

Sindell, Milo.
      The end of work as you know it : 8 strategies to redefine work on your
  terms / Milo Sindell and Thuy Sindell. — 1st ed.
          p.   cm.
      Summary: "A new career approach for employees who want to make
  their jobs work for them instead of the other way around"—Provided by
  publisher.
      1. Job satisfaction. 2. Quality of work life. 3. Career development.
  I. Sindell, Thuy. II. Title.
  HF5549.5.J63S477 2009
  650.1—dc22   2009024949

ISBN 978-1-58008-997-5

Printed in the United States of America

Cover design by Ed Anderson
Text design by Jeff Brandenburg

10   9   8   7   6   5   4   3   2   1

First Edition

CONTENTS

ACKNOWLEDGMENTS

We'd like to thank our agent, Kimberley Cameron, for seeing the possibilities for how this piece of work will change people's lives and their experience of work. We'd also like to thank the Ten Speed team for getting behind the book and bringing it to life. Finally, we'd like to thank all the people we've encountered in our personal and professional lives who have influenced us and were the inspiration for this book.

And especially to Ava, who has brought an unprecedented depth, meaning, and love into our lives.

PREFACE

The contemporary workplace is dynamic, fickle, and complex. We spend the bulk of our waking hours living and breathing work. Given the amount of time spent on the job, shouldn't we get what we want from the experience? There's no need to drag yourself out of bed every morning to face another day filled with stress and frustrating colleagues. Work is ideally a place where you gain a sense of achievement and alignment between who you are and what you do. The workplace is fertile ground to achieve personal goals, manifest the values that you hold important, and create a sense of deep accomplishment.

Idealistic? Yes. Realistic? We believe so. It is easy to dismiss the workplace with Dilbert-like sarcasm. Even we can easily find ourselves taking a negative tone about workplace relations. We have worked for and consulted to some of the best-known companies and can safely say that politics, stupidity, and the worst of human nature is very much a part of the work landscape. The challenge and opportunity lie not just in finding the good in your job but—much more important—in discovering alignment between who you are and what you do.

In our first book, *Sink or Swim*, we wanted to guide new hires step-by-step to ensure their success. Our second book, *Job Spa*, soon followed because we recognized the need for a book that guided employees to become more engaged in their current jobs by taking more accountability for their success and looking for the opportunities to both give more to and take more from their work. Then we realized that instead of helping people become more engaged with work, we could help prevent them from being disengaged from the start. If we can help people create a workday experience in which they know they will be stimulated and they are achieving the goals they set for themselves, it will no longer feel like work. Seventy-one percent disengagement in the workplace (according to Gallup, 2004) will no longer be a reality.

Most of us feel disconnected from our work because we work not for ourselves and our dreams and goals, but for our company's goals. The following story is an example of how this disconnect is propagated and reinforced in our society today.

In June 2007, we attended the graduation ceremony of four thousand newly minted East Coast Ivy-Leaguers. Before us was a crowd of bright-eyed students, eager to pass over the threshold of college into the world. We were looking at the future. The excitement was contagious.

Like most attendees, we were looking forward to the keynote, which was going to be delivered by a local professional sports coach. Giving a keynote to a group of knowledge-filled, get-me-out-of-here, soon-to-be-grads is not easy. Handing them warmed-over platitudes is a minimum expectation. We did not expect too much enlightenment. Fortunately, our levels of surprise and amusement were about to be spiked.

The fearless keynoter started off framing for our eager grads the habits and character critical to every soon-to-be employee's success. As he transitioned to a story about food, our attention perked up. The story took the all-American breakfast—bacon and eggs—and turned it into the worst of budding new employee brainwash. As we listened, the speaker transformed "bacon and eggs" into the litmus test of character and *the* choice for our new grads to make.

According to our speaker, there are two types of people: chickens and pigs. On the one hand, the chicken just lays its eggs, provides a product for anyone's breakfast, and keeps on clucking. Its commitment is passing. We listened, awestruck. As a "chicken employee," the coach explained, you are in it for yourself. The pig, on the other hand, is truly committed. There is no going back once the bacon is on the plate. "Pig employees" commit to the employers unwaveringly.

As grads transitioning into the world of work, the speaker continued, you have to decide whether you are one of the chickens who are working for companies on their own (the chicken's) terms, or one of the pigs, who are willing to commit all the way. The speaker insisted that good employees are pigs. Are you a pig?

We were amazed. What an incredibly unhealthy expectation to place on anyone, especially an audience of bright, motivated fledglings entering the world of work.

You've probably heard some variation on this story, in which you were told that a good employee listens to the boss and stays loyal to the company despite its shortcomings. Promoting the idea that a good employee blindly commits to the company and job is mind-boggling. This choice is not only dangerous and naive for the employee, but also not in the best interest of the employer. As an employee, first and foremost, you need to commit to *your* success. Self-commitment is the prime principle of a long and fortuitous career. Similarly, employers need workers who are clear on their contribution, agile enough to move with change, and not rigidly fixated on a blind commitment that has outlived its use. The right balance is a full-time commitment to your own success and an evolving commitment to a series of employers, depending on your career needs.

We have committed our careers to helping every working individual find their raison d'être and voice. Work should be an outlet for you to achieve your professional goals. It's tragic that most people begin and continue throughout their lifetime to work without understanding what they truly want from the experience. Most people blindly commit and follow. The "bacon and eggs" story plays itself out again and again. There is so much more potential to achieve great things as part of your job than choosing which barnyard animal represents your inner employee.

When there is harmony between what you do, why you do it, and the results you achieve, you have created the end of work as you know it. Why would you want to create your end of work? If you see work as a means to an end (that is to say, a paycheck or résumé builder), you probably feel trapped—maybe even resentful that you have to go to work. If you want to feel more positive toward the experience of work, you've got to figure out what's in it for you beyond a paycheck. When you do, you will have discovered the end of work as you know it. Work will take on a different meaning for you.

At a macro level, this book will help you see what you do professionally in a new way. It will guide you to make powerful choices and create greater alignment between who you are and what you do for a living. At the day-to-day level, you will discover the tools to get back on track when you find yourself disengaged and frustrated with work.

In the following pages, we offer you the opportunity to claim your professional autonomy, helping you to find freedom through choice, define what you want to achieve, and shape your perspective to accomplish what you want in the places you work throughout your life.

WHY CREATE YOUR END OF WORK?

> Find something you love to do and you will never
> work a day in your life.
>
> —MARK TWAIN

Imagine you won the lottery—not just one of those scratcher cards, but the big one. You've won enough to set you up for the rest of your life. We bet one of the first decisions you would make, even before deciding to build that media room you've always dreamed of, would be to retire. Then, after spending a few months bathing in your newfound wealth, you would eventually come to a point at which something uniquely human begins to bubble up. At first, you might ignore this sensation. Naggingly, the sensation returns, to become a constant din in the back of your mind: a desire to do something, to contribute, to be challenged, to experience the feeling of being able to point to something and say, "I made that!" But you wouldn't jump back into that gray polyester-lined cubicle in the accounting department that you just left. No—now, you have options.

Although you have been launched into the upper stratosphere of income statistics, you are still swimming in the human gene pool and can't escape the coding that connects us all—the desire to create and contribute. You feel this need to do something with your life. Your immediate thought is to go back to work. Only this time, you would work on your own terms.

Does this scenario sound nuts to you? Research over the last sixty years has consistently reported that a majority of people would want to work even if they didn't have to. Specifically, researchers in multiple studies posed the question, "Would you still continue working if you inherited a large set-for-life sum, won the lottery, or suddenly came upon the means to not need to work for the money?" The results were consistent. In each study, approximately 70 percent responded that they would still work. Ironically, the Gallup organization states that approximately seven out of ten employees are not happy with their work. Why is there is a such a huge disconnect between our desire to work and our enjoyment of work?

Psychologist Mihaly Csikszentmihalyi suggests that there is an underlying tension when we feel that our time and energy are spent fulfilling the goals of others. We agree. This tension—sometimes unconscious, other times like a neon sign in our minds—undermines our motivation. Why shouldn't it? Can someone be expected to wake up at six in the morning, drive an hour or more to work, and spend their day on an objective that has no inherent link to what is important to them, *without* feeling tension? We wrote this book to help you relieve this tension. By understanding the choices that you can make, you will be better equipped to fulfill what is important to you through your work.

Our jobs—what we do or create—can contribute to our sense of identity and of being a contributor to something larger than ourselves. In addition, the feeling of accomplishment from a job well done is universal. And the feeling of defeat and frustration when there is emptiness in our efforts is also universal. On a deeper level, when the results of our labor do not reflect who we are and what we want, a fundamental part of us as human beings is not nourished.

Work can bring fulfillment; in great workplaces, it is a conduit for the best of the human spirit. No matter the economic climate or workplace, finding this potential is always important. In the face of economic transformation, challenge, and an unforeseen future, the value of each person's exploring, finding, and owning what brings them meaning in the work they do is critical. When you are clear on your relationship to your job, you are better able to draw strength, stay focused, and make decisions based on something much more substantial than a reaction. In steadier times, the same is true: comfort, routine, and ease are enemies that can prevent you from making decisions that, although they may challenge you, are more aligned with who you are and your values. No matter what the current economic situation is, we all feel the need to understand who we are and to align our efforts with that truth in our work.

The concept of employment and work has come full circle from 350 years ago. From farmers and tradespeople, who owned their production (produced a good and sold a good), through the transformation of the industrial and technological revolutions, we have returned to a time of "ownership." Most of us are not farmers who sell our crops or tradespeople who sell our wares. We are individuals who can transition from company to company and sell our knowledge and skills. We have mobility and options because we have ownership of our knowledge and skills. We want to also acknowledge that there have been many brave people who have followed their entrepreneurial spirit. While that spirit is to be admired, this is not always an option for others due to personality and personal circumstances. Thus, a lot of us still choose to work for others, which reinforces the tension we feel and why this book is so important. There has been a liberation from our former dependence on only what our hands can produce to the freedom of using our capacity for ideas, knowledge, and technical acumen. A renaissance of possibilities and potential is now to be found in the choices we can make.

Create the Path to Your End of Work

In this book, we present eight strategies, each of which can lead you to a fundamental difference in how you experience work. Given that we are each unique, you will find some of these strategies more appropriate than others. As you read, remember this: *Each strategy is equal to the rest in its potential to be effective.* Some of these strategies may readily resonate with you now and reflect an immediate need. Others may be more effective at different times in your life. Each strategy, if right for you, can affect you on a life-changing level or on a daily basis and lead to your true success in the workplace. Focus on one or as many as necessary to reframe your experience of work and create your personal end of work.

SETTING THE STAGE

Before you jump into your workplace adventure, you need to consider a few important items. When it comes to the workplace, career, and your end of work exploration, there are a number of subtle and not-so-subtle emotional elements. Let's first consider two potential emotional barriers to reaching your end of work: your feelings of *happiness* and *worthiness*.

First, know that the purpose of achieving your end of work is not happiness. Your end of work offers a whole lot more than simple happiness. In fact, your end of work is everything else *but* happiness. Why? Happiness is one of those broad umbrella emotions, like anger. Happiness and anger are given way too much emphasis, as they are fantastic covers for our more complex feelings. People spend so much time wanting simply to be happy without understanding what happiness actually means to them. We think we want to be happy at work, in our relationships, in our careers, and our lives. Sounds nice, except for the fact that happiness doesn't just suddenly appear. To get there, you need to know what lies within your definition of happiness.

Your ideal work environment and end of work may have nothing to do with happiness. Do you really go through your day seeking happiness? We hope not. When you think about it, you'll realize that you probably go through your day seeking to be curious, challenged, recognized, appreciated, creative, or satisfied. The culmination of these states of being may result in sporadic shots of happiness, but happiness as a constant state of being? Is that possible or even desirable? Think for a moment beyond happy. Consider what brings you "happiness." Look closer at how the various aspects of your life generate specific emotional responses. By discovering and living these aspects, you will gain much richer and more dynamic professional experiences.

Second, you must believe that you are worthy of achieving exactly what you want. At the very least, you must temporarily suppress any undermining thoughts. The end of work is about calling your own shots. If you don't believe you deserve great things, you'll find it tough to make them happen. We provide some encouragement throughout the book to ensure that you cruise though this potential roadblock to reach end of work success.

With a deeper understanding of what lies beneath your "happiness," and with confirmation that you are worthy of what you want to achieve, you already have 99 percent of what is required to achieve your end of work. In addition to the talents you already possess, we want to call out a couple more. The eight strategies you will explore require autofocus skills, specifically:

> **Zoom Out.** The ability to step out and see how a strategy plays out on a larger scale over the course of a job, career, and lifetime.

> **Zoom In.** The ability to get close up to see the day-to-day connections of a strategy in action.

These skills help you think through a choice: how that choice plays out day-to-day and week-to-week, and ultimately sustains itself over time. These autofocus skills are vital to help you think through the actions you will take to make your choice a reality.

INTRODUCING THE EIGHT END OF WORK STRATEGIES

Each chapter focuses on one of these eight strategies, with an overview and specific steps you can take if you decide that strategy is right for you. There is no right or wrong strategy, and no right number of strategies to try. The right strategy for you today may not work for you a decade from now. Why? If you are at a relatively early point in your career, you may find that certain things such as learning new skills and advancing your career are more important to you. If you are midcareer, you may find that being recognized by your organization for hard work is a rarity and therefore what you need right now. And if you are in the later stages of your career, you may find that you are thinking about the lasting impact and contributions you have made to your organization and industry. The strategy choices are different for different people at different times in their lives.

1. **Share Expertise:** Put yourself on retainer with benefits! Your company is now your client. Make yourself available to your client as part of your normal workweek to provide your skills and wisdom. Manage your energy for maximum results for you and your company.

2. **Initiate Change:** Stop complaining! Become an agent for change when you see an opportunity to make something better. Identify what you can do to influence change within the organization and system.

3. **Demand Autonomy:** Declare your own rebellion! Don't depend on others for your success. Get clear on your demands and objectives and take accountability for your career.

4. **Create Meaning:** Wake up! Emerge from what has seemed a blurry, dreamlike state of the work routine into lucidity. Discover how to transcend the bland and maximize the potential of the great opportunities around you.

5. **Spark Creativity:** Become an artist! Make your work environment a place to create, explore, and innovate.

6. **Seize Recognition:** Take a bow! Identify your audiences. Define what you want to accomplish, and gain the recognition you deserve.

7. **Maintain Balance:** Set your boundaries! It's time to step away from weekend office work, email addiction, and sixteen-hour workdays. Decide what you need to do to take care of yourself.

8. **Build Legacy:** Leave your mark! Create something that has an impact on the companies you work with. Define not only what you want to leave behind, but also what you want to take with you for all your years of service.

When you choose a strategy (or several) and follow through, you will find that:

- The conversations you have with coworkers, at all levels, will shift because you are clear on your trajectory to achieving your end of work.

- You will know what you want to give to the companies you work with and what you expect in return.

- You will know what companies you do or do not want to be a part of.

- You will be more selective in the projects and jobs you take because you will have a deeper awareness of what opportunities, environments, and challenges are best for you.

- The conversations you have with prospective employers will shift; you will interview companies versus companies interviewing you.

- When you start a new job, you will make an impact more quickly and decode the culture more effectively because you look at your new environment through a lens that reflects what you want and the intentional choices you make.

Let's get started!

1

SHARE
EXPERTISE

After two years on the job at his PR firm, Philip was slowly becoming frustrated that new projects and opportunities were not happening quickly enough. Maybe, he thought, it was time to move on to a new company. He was spending too much time waiting for the firm to use his knowledge. He took a step back and decided to no longer be a victim. Although he wasn't working sixty hours a week like at his last job, he was certainly underutilized by his current employer. Philip determined how he could take initiative to share his knowledge with others in the company. He also realized that in his current situation he was working fewer hours and getting paid more money. Isn't this what he wanted anyway? Philip concluded, "Hmmm. More money, fewer hours, and it's like I am a consultant on retainer sharing my expertise when the company needs it."

Liberate yourself by making the shift from indentured employee to expert on retainer. Share Expertise to use what you know, maximize your effectiveness, and manage your energy. You have a unique and specific set of skills and knowledge. This is why your company employs you.

Is This Strategy Right for You? The Share Expertise strategy is likely to work for you if

- You feel confident you've got what it takes.

- You're ready to contribute your expertise to provide solutions.

- You enjoy continually sharpening your skills.

- You want to position your skills so they'll be put to maximum use.

When to Apply: Breathe a fresh and liberating perspective into your work. It's time to recalibrate your expectations of your job—what you give, how you give, and what you expect in return. Share Expertise to manage your expectations of your work and to maximize your unique skills and knowledge.

What Sharing Expertise Will Do for You: Sharing expertise will help you to effectively contribute what you know, reevaluate your relationship with your work, and appreciate your workplace in a whole new way. You'll experience a transformative shift from simply being an employee to redefining yourself as a paid expert. You will feel liberated because you will contribute on your terms. Making this choice will also help you save and manage your energy for when you need to step up and put your knowledge, skills, and talents to use.

Do you go to work feeling like the knowledge you bring is not always used by your employer? Does it seem that, although you are engaged and motivated, only a small percentage of what you have to offer is used? Maybe you feel tired of extending yourself—volunteering for projects, suggesting new initiatives, and working way too hard, yet not reaping the rewards. Sometimes you need to step back, evaluate the true value of what you bring to your job, and identify the most efficient way to contribute—even if it means working less.

What Is Expertise?

Imagine a world of work where you get paid for your ideas. In fact, people depend on you to share your expertise with them. Wouldn't that be a great world in which to exist? Wait a minute—you already work there! That's what you are paid for: contributing your ideas and knowledge at work. It is challenging to have this perspective when your work environment feels out of your control: customer demands, team dynamics, market shifts, projects that come and go, and demands that are placed on you can push you from too much down time to no time to think. What if you stepped out of your current perspective and put yourself in the driver's seat? For a growing number of people, their workplace is viewed as a customer; they are available to that customer when and how they are needed: as experts on retainer. As hired experts, they share their expertise to their employer when and how it is required. In making this shift, your perspective changes from floating adrift in the demands of your workplace to a self-defined relationship with your work.

In the context of this little book, *expertise* is defined as having a body of knowledge, perspective, or methods that are transferable. You have expertise. Recognize yourself as someone who has unique and useful ideas to contribute to others. Most of us assume that expertise is defined as having a depth of knowledge in one particular area. Although this is true, for the purpose of creating your end of work as you know it, we expand on this definition to include "unique and useful knowledge"—because everyone has ideas to contribute. Each idea is unique, because we all have different experiences that color the lens through which we view the world. As such, each idea holds possibilities. Each idea has value.

Share Expertise is a strategy to manage and deploy your ideas and add value to your organization. Granted, every day will not always be an expertise day. Sometimes it's going to be "organize your files day" or "empty out your email inbox day," which are the mundane tasks of even the most exciting job. Other days, you will be asked to be the hero or take initiative to jump in and save the day with a great solution that draws on your expertise. Therefore, consider yourself on retainer. You'll be called on for your expertise when needed.

Our expert, Philip, wanted his capabilities to be put to maximum use by the organization. He wanted to make great contributions on a regular basis to feel like he was adding value. He wanted to add value regularly because it gave him a sense of accomplishment, but his expectations were not realistic, given shifting company priorities, a chaotic work environment, and a chorus of other employees seeking attention. What the company needed was for Philip to be generally reliable and engaged and, when they needed him to be a star, to step up and perform admirably. Once Philip understood that this process was about the organization's timing, not their judgment of his worth, it liberated him to see himself in a different light. He was an expert on retainer. This shift in how he saw himself and his role enabled him to be less focused on competing for attention, less personally attached to a single soon-to-be reprioritized initiative. He would instead focus on what he could control and where he could add real value.

This particular definition of expertise is intended to shift our current paradigm for how we see ourselves and our contribution to our employer. Not every moment at work is going to be a career-defining moment. Sometimes, as employees, we become "defining-moment junkies." We want every moment and every day at work to feel like a rush. Although this could be exciting, it's not necessary or realistic. If you see yourself as an expert on retainer, you shift to acceptance of being the hero and getting the rush *only* when needed by the organization, not because you need it every day. Even the most high-achieving experts need slow days to regroup, catch their breath, and even refresh their expertise in a subject.

The Principles of the Share Expertise Strategy

Here are three principles to help reinforce your expertise perspective.

First, you need to *define what knowledge, experiences, and insights make your ideas and contributions unique.* Then look to see *when you can impart this unique knowledge* so that it's most useful to your organization. Finally, *determine how to manage your contribution* through a targeted effort.

Here's a deeper dive into the three principles.

1. **What knowledge, experiences, and insights do I hold that make my ideas and contributions unique?** Most of us have followed a singular path to reach our current situation in our job and career. What was your path? What training, courses, degrees, or certifications did you pick up along the way? What projects did you get involved in? What did you learn from those experiences? What were the politics of the people and organizations with whom you've worked? What insights did you gain about how best to get things accomplished, given those complexities? No one else has had your exact experience. The insights you've gained in the course of your career contribute to the knowledge you bring to the table. This is extremely valuable information that you can in turn contribute to your organization.

Philip grew up in a household with a father who was a doctor, a mother who was a homemaker, and three other siblings. He earned a degree in communications and studied abroad for a year while in college. He worked for several marketing firms before joining this public relations firm. He decided to make the switch because he wanted to grow into a related area to round out his experience, and also to challenge himself to build on his prior skills and apply them in a different arena. His background, upbringing, degree, international experience, and marketing background all enrich his perspective. They are what make his ideas and contributions uniquely his.

2. **When to impart unique knowledge.** Experts know exactly when to apply their ideas. As an expert, you are keenly aware of the organizational state of your company and what it needs from you. Something relevant and useful is much more valuable than an outside or uninformed view because of the level of impact it can have for the organization at that particular time. This is not about your ego—this is what the organization needs. Experts are fully aware of this.

Never short of ideas, Philip was quick to come up with new angles and fresh client pitches. It frustrated him that although his ideas were acknowledged, often they were not acted on. Isn't that what he was hired to do? Not just to make proposals, but also to implement the solutions? What was going on? His initial response was to blame himself and dwell on a growing self-perception that he was not living up to expectations. It was not until a check-in meeting with his boss, in which he shared his concern, that he realized he was overanalyzing the situation. His boss said he loved his contributions and was fine with the fact that clients did not always move beyond recommendation to implementation. Philip finally realized that this pattern was not about him; rather, it was about the organizational state of flux and the client's timing, so he quickly got over his doubts. He would still put 100 percent into his work. The difference is that now he will manage his assumptions and effort by first ascertaining what he can provide and deliver when and as needed—as opposed to constantly going above and beyond, overextending himself, and making assumptions about what his company and the client needed him to provide.

3. **Manage your contribution through a targeted effort.** Experts understand the environment and landscape of their workplace. As such, they manage their contributions accordingly. They identify the needs of the people around them—this could include a boss who wants to demonstrate competence and have a high-performing team,

coworkers who want to look good and do the right thing by the organization, and a department that is struggling to achieve its goals with limited resources. By understanding these dynamics, an expert is able to determine whether contributing ideas about process improvement or ideas about new initiatives would be most valuable to the organization. By creating a category by which to define your organization, you are able to look at your contributions through that particular lens and determine what to contribute and when.

For Philip, being more targeted in sharing his expertise meant that he would keep in mind the state of his organization and the client's needs at all times. Philip created categories he noticed about his clients' needs: "cool and innovative," "sure wins," and "biggest bang for the buck." Depending on the needs of his clients, he saw the problems and solutions much more clearly and was able to contribute more effectively. This left him with a much more satisfying experience of work.

Why Share Expertise?

It can be really frustrating working for an organization that doesn't seem to be efficient and effective at using your skills. You may feel like you are firing on half of your cylinders most of the time. Though it may not seem to bother your employers that they are not getting their money's worth, you still feel bored and underutilized. The only way for you to stay engaged and feel good about being at your company is to share expertise when it's needed. This is the best way to reframe your experience so that you don't get frustrated and can manage your energy. The good news for both you and your company is that when you manage your energy using your expert perspective, you make the most of the opportunity when the time comes to add your input.

Additionally, the experience of getting worked up and frustrated is not worth the emotional roller-coaster ride. At the end of the day, the sun still sets in the same place, and your organization is not going to change how it fundamentally operates. You can choose to get sucked into the drama and politics of that or to see yourself as an expert on retainer. You get paid for maintaining a certain level of performance, and every now and then you are asked to step up and contribute your phenomenal ideas. That's the beauty of being on retainer: you get to be a hero when your clients need you—which will probably not be every day.

Is the Share Expertise Strategy Right for You?

Expertise is a reflection of the unique knowledge, experiences, and insights you bring to the table only when needed; think *energy management*. You are an engine of potential that, when appropriate, will unleash your horsepower. Use the following criteria to determine whether this is the right strategy for you to create your end of work:

- *You've got what it takes.* You've worked hard on earning your degree(s), achieving your certifications, getting trained, and doing your research. You've lived through many reorganizations in your career. You've dealt with company politics and the nasty sharks that have infested the waters. You've endured unkind managers and appreciated kind ones. You've earned your marks. The title of expert is yours. You've held back; now it's your time to shine. You've got something to say. If you are ready to step up and claim your part as the expert in your team, department, or organization, then Share Expertise is the right strategy for you.

- *You're ready to contribute your expertise to provide solutions.* If you are tired of hearing others talk about their ideas when you know that yours are better, then Share Expertise is the right strategy for you. You've been sitting on the sidelines. You know your solutions are more comprehensive, better thought through, and more effective at yielding both short- and long-term results. You are ready to make that contribution to your organization.

- *You enjoy continually sharpening your skills.* If you like to learn and constantly hone your skills, then Share Expertise is the right strategy for you. You take the time to invest in your skills. You enroll yourself in courses and take advantage of organizational trainings. You get excited by learning something new. You take pride in your abilities. With all the investments you've made in yourself, you are sitting on quite a bit of knowledge and expertise that could be put to good use.

- *You want to position your skills so they'll be put to maximum use.* If you want to be used for what you know, then Share Expertise is the right strategy for you.

If any of these four descriptions sound like you, use the Share Expertise strategy to help you create the end of work as you know it (to find out how, read on). Your Share Expertise strategy will help you define your knowledge and find useful ways in which to make significant contributions while managing your efforts and collecting a full-time paycheck.

Make Expertise a Reality

We've explored the definition and underlying principles of expertise. Now that you've determined that the Share Expertise strategy is an effective one for you to use to create the end of work as you know it, we will explore how to bring your Share Expertise strategy to life by first defining your knowledge and how it would be useful to others, then creating an action plan to make this strategy a reality.

DEFINE YOUR EXPERTISE

We've discussed Philip's unique knowledge of marketing and how his background and experience in having studied abroad have contributed to the way he sees the world. He has defined his expertise as the totality of what he brings to the table: an international perspective on what the markets want to read about in the media. He's come to see himself as an expert on retainer. If there's a client need that has an international dimension, then that's where he can fully contribute his expertise. That's not to suggest he doesn't jump into other projects that don't have a similarly international element. Philip just doesn't see himself as an expert in those projects, so he's less attached when there are disagreements among the team. Not every battle is worth fighting. This has helped him become more effective at pitching the right ideas at the right time. Now, use this section to define *your* expertise and how it can be useful to your organization.

First, you're going to zoom out. Take a step back and reflect on who you are and where you've been. What was your upbringing and how does this continue to affect your worldview? What kind of formal coursework and training have you had, and how does this inform the work you do? What kinds of positive and negative experiences have you had with coworkers and organizations, and how has this impacted the way you might interpret a situation or problem and possible solutions? When you look at the gestalt of who you are and your experiences, what makes your knowledge stand out? Take a moment to reflect on this and write down what comes to mind.

For instance, let's say you've accumulated solid experience working in a start-up environment; now you find yourself at a new company, which is confronting a dilemma about a product release date. Determine how confidently you understand the nuances of the founders' concerns (because of your previous start-up experience) and confirm that the team really needs to complete the project for on-time release versus missing the deadline for the sake of increased quality. After all, the next version can be quickly released without many people noticing the few bugs. Your expertise can be demonstrated by stating your understanding of both perspectives and why your experience and knowledge about your product and customers has led you to side with the founders. First to market will be key to your success given the competition. This is what makes you an expert. No one can take that away from you.

Now here's the second part. Given that you've identified your area of expertise, let's determine how and when you want to contribute your expertise. For Philip, this meant scaling back from full-speed, maximum, 24/7 contribution—a sure recipe for both feeling underappreciated and burning out. He determined that a more strategic tack would help ensure that the best of his talents were used and his contribution recognized. One action that Philip now takes to manage his effort is creating a mental criteria list for projects and initiatives he wants to pursue. For instance, this list includes international issues and communities. Anytime there's a project with an international dimension (or a project where that dimension should be present), Philip sees it as an opportunity to bring forth his passion and expertise around those issues. Instead of throwing himself into every project and burning out because he's trying to fight uphill battles in which he's not necessarily the expert, he now ensures that he is maximizing his time, effort, and contribution. He's an expert when he needs to be, and is less attached to the outcomes of certain projects. That doesn't mean Philip is less engaged—he's simply more selective about which projects he pours his heart and soul into.

When you take a look at your team, department, and organization, what is its current state? Specifically, what is the resource situation (budget and headcount), political situation, and morale level? How are these various aspects affecting the team, department, and organization? Given this state, how does this affect what your colleagues perceive as important? Given their priorities, what kinds of solutions would be helpful? Where can your expertise be best used by the company? This affects how and when you gear up to be an expert. Ideally, the organization should be using your expertise at all times to get a full return on their money, but given the nature of organizations and the constant state of change and flux, it is unrealistic to assume that your expertise will be needed at all times. Outline the criteria you see for what kind of expertise, when this expertise, and how this expertise can be best shared. For example, in our earlier start-up example, it was crucial to understand product marketing and positioning. When situations come up about the product features, pricing, release dates, and quality, a person with expertise will be sure to contribute. The best way to share expertise is not to come across as a know-it-all and turn people off from one's opinions. If you are truly confident of your expertise, you can be willing to seek understanding of other people's opinions when there is a disagreement instead of claiming expertise to end the conversation.

YOUR SHARE EXPERTISE ACTIONS

Now that you've chosen to make Share Expertise your strategy and defined your expertise, it's time to make it a reality. Let's look at the attitude and actions that will bring them to life. This section explores ways in which you can zoom out to shift your attitude and zoom in to take actions to make sharing expertise your reality.

First consider the following principles. Your attitude influences your actions. The greatest possible hindrance to success is your attitude. Therefore, to create the end of work as you know it, you must start with the right attitude.

Here are three key points to keep in mind:

1. **You have good ideas.** There are no silly ideas. Your ideas come from a place of knowledge, experience, and insights that are unique to you as a person. You must believe that your ideas have value in order for others to believe that they have value.

2. **You have ideas worth sharing.** Although you may have good ideas, they are no good to anyone if you don't share them. Don't hold back. Stop the little voice in the back of your head that keeps you from speaking up. If you believe that others need to hear what you have to say because it's worth their time and energy, then they will listen.

3. **Don't give up.** Your ideas are great. Sometimes they may not hit the mark; other times your timing may be off. This doesn't mean that you are no longer the expert you pride yourself in being. Timing and luck can sometimes be a more important factor than the content of your ideas. Consider that everyone around you is thinking about his or her own priorities, perspectives, and deadlines; it's not realistic to expect them to stop and cheer each time you lob out a new idea. Ensuring that your ideas are heard will require a consistent effort.

Where should you apply your newfound attitude? Revisit your list of ideas about your expertise and how you can apply it. How do these three key points affect the way you will go about expressing your expertise? Will you trust that you'll come across as more confident and stronger when you judiciously choose when to provide your expertise? Will you not allow yourself to get frustrated and give up if people don't understand your ideas right away? Will you table it and try again when the time is right?

First, let's look at your current projects. What are the areas in which you can increase the delivery of your expertise? Are there areas in which you've been holding back, or areas for which you have been providing ideas, but you haven't incorporated all of your background, experience, and observations to craft the most effective solution? Take stock of what you've been working on and create the space to introduce your expertise in a more deliberate manner. For instance, in our start-up example (see page 9), an expert would have tried to bring her expertise to the table to solve the product release issue. She would have created an opportunity to leverage and engage the first wave of adopters or even beta testers to actually find bugs on behalf of the company and somehow make it fun or competitive, like challenging them to break the system.

Second, let's take a look at your team and the larger organization. Similarly, what are some areas in which you can contribute your expertise? In the context of this evaluation, how have your previous contributions have been effective—or failed to produce your hoped-for results? Moving forward, you will want to target both the likeliest opportunities to contribute as well as the methods most likely to be effective.

Finally, what additional areas of expertise would you like to develop? That is, what training, coursework, or projects would you like to be involved in that will help you expand your breadth and depth of experience and information? For example, our start-up expert could have decided that she wanted to leverage her start-up situation to learn more about venture capital funding and how to maneuver the financial challenges a small company faces. Create a list of the additional things you want to learn and start to look at ways in which you can bring these experiences into your life.

As a result of bringing your expertise into reality, you may feel like you are doing less. This can be a significant adjustment for people who are used to overachieving. Again, think in terms of energy management. Your goal is not to do less; in fact, you are doing more, just in a targeted manner. You are not spinning your wheels trying to make contributions that are not wanted and tying your sense of worth to that futile effort. Now, as a "consultant on retainer," you are an expert who will be called on when needed.

Clarify your areas of expertise and determine where it makes the most sense to make your contributions. People who choose Share Expertise as their strategy for creating their end of work are clear about the value of their contribution. Their value as a person and employee is not tied to how the organization uses them. It's tied to what they choose to contribute and how they choose to contribute their knowledge. You may have good ideas about how to solve a problem, but if you aren't being asked for your ideas, they may fall on deaf ears. Timing is everything. A consultant on retainer understands this and uses it to her advantage. That's how the Share Expertise strategy works to create the end of work as you know it.

2

INITIATE
CHANGE

After nine months on the job, Mary began to get a better sense of how things worked at her new company. Struck by the disconnect between the stated values of innovation and collaboration and the ongoing complaints from employees about the lack of public space where coworkers could meet outside of their offices and just hang out, Mary decided to see what she could do. Specifically, the company needed space where employees could congregate to brainstorm and have impromptu meetings. The company said it valued innovation, but the endless rows of gray cubicles only limited co-worker contact. Mary figured, "Why not try to create change as opposed to complaining about what's not working?" Mary took the initiative to gather support for her idea and created a committee made up of company leaders. This committee devised a plan and got senior management approval to build an on-site cafeteria and create informal meeting areas to encourage employees to get out of their cubicles and talk to each other more. Although taking initiative to drive change could have been risky for someone who had been on the job for less than a year, Mary seized the opportunity to take action where others only saw problems.

If something's not working, step up. Become an agent for change. Sometimes it is up to you to make a difference. Initiate Change to move from being an observer or critic to being an activist. Instead of checking out, become an engaged part of your environment. Use your strengths, be a champion for change, help others, and fight for the causes you care most about.

Is This Strategy Right for You? Initiate Change is a good strategy for you if

- You're ready to move beyond complaints to action.
- You long to apply your skills and talents to standing up for what you believe in and making a difference.
- You'd like to be more engaged with your work environment.
- You have knowledge of the system that you could effectively use to change it for the better.

When to Apply: Initiate Change when it's time to make a difference, when you are on the verge of checking out, and when you see an opportunity to create something new.

What Initiating Change Will Do for You: This strategy will help you become an advocate and use your knowledge of the system that you are a part of. Your Initiate Change strategy will transform you from an observer to an active participant and problem solver. This strategy will help you learn how to identify important issues, solve problems, influence others, build relationships, and reinforce your talents and skills.

Do you tire of hearing yourself or others complain about the same problems over and over again? Some problems can appear so monumental that it seems difficult to make an impact. Other problems are solvable, but require some effort. When you think about your workplace, what problems do you see for which there are clear solutions—and what are you doing to bring them about? We can become so absorbed in our projects and tasks that sometimes we forget that the things that make work difficult can be solved with a bit of initiative. Once that barrier is removed, work becomes easier and more enjoyable. Initiate change when you see the opportunity to make something better.

What Is Change?

Imagine a workplace where everything made sense. There is no bureaucracy. There are no backward procedures and outdated technology. Your work day is fluid, and you are able to accomplish your tasks. That kind of workplace can exist, but it requires people who believe things can be better and who strive to make it so. No matter what your motivation is, by choosing Initiate Change as your end of work strategy you are no longer an observer. You are now a participant.

Bringing about change requires you to take the risk of disturbing the status quo. Most people are change-averse. If given the choice between an uncomfortable but familiar situation and an unknown yet potentially better situation, most people will choose the familiar. The opportunity to make something better through a change may be challenging, but with these challenges comes excitement. In fact, initiating change keeps you engaged and on your toes.

Our Initiate Change expert, Mary, was clear that things could be better. Instead of being frustrated by the disconnect between company values and workplace setup, she saw this as an opportunity to improve the work environment. Her coworkers had gotten used to just complaining and experiencing their workplace as "the way things are" in the company. This was a challenge Mary was willing to take on. She found it exciting to see how much she could change the physical work environment and affect the quality of life in her new company. Mary also knew she couldn't be a maverick and just go make it happen. Effective change requires understanding the issues and players, potential supporters and opposing forces, and having a plan for action. She needed to understand whether there was any specific historical reason behind the setup of the space, make a compelling case for change, and enroll the support of key executives. Mary needed more than a goal and a plan. She needed to understand the organizational landscape.

The Principles of the Initiate Change Strategy

Two core principles define and propel the Initiate Change strategy. First, you need to *see your environment through the lens of potential improvements*. From there, opportunities will present themselves, and when they do, it is important to *be curious*. Why are things the way they are? What will it take to make things better? In this section, we look at the principles of the Initiate Change strategy as part of your overall strategy to create your end of work. Later in the chapter, we will discuss the steps involved in implementing change.

1. **Improvements.** When you see your work environment through the lens of potential improvements, you'll realize that the opportunities are endless. One could say everything can be improved. As such, you will need to prioritize and strategically select your causes. Which ones can you most readily improve? What changes are important to you and to others, and why? What changes will meet resistance? Determine where your strengths lie in relationship to a selected change. This includes skills, tools, and relationships that will help you make the change a reality.

As a new employee, Mary saw everything from a fresh perspective. The opportunities for improvement were boundless: from the lack of a cafeteria to the impaired internal communication to the lack of public space. But there are limited hours in a day, so Mary had to pick the one challenge she felt most passionate about—the one where she felt she could make a positive impact.

Over the course of nine months, she developed relationships with people in different departments, including human resources and facilities. These relationships would prove useful when she pitched her ideas.

2. **Curiosity.** Underlying a desire to create change is a *sense of curiosity* for how something could be different, better, easier, more efficient. Buoying this curiosity is a *desire for action*. Curiosity without a desire for action is only passive inquiry. So what does the curiosity of the change advocate look like? It involves asking questions about what could be better and exploring the history of why things are done a certain way, the concerns if things were to change, and what "better" would look like. It is important to not just ask questions but also understand the range of perspectives from people who will be involved or affected by the change. Taking time to understand multiple views demonstrates that you are genuine in your desire to make improvements, and not driving your own personal agenda for an individual win.

For Mary, the need for public spaces in the company was blatantly obvious from day one. She was hired from another company that was known for being innovative. Although she knew she was being asked to bring her ideas and experience to her new job, she was not being asked to explicitly address the lack of communal work areas. So she took her time asking questions to understand the culture and history of the company. How long had they been in the current space? What did the former spaces look like? Who designed the current office layout? What was their thinking? She explored her assumption that the company truly did want to drive innovation in a number of ways, including the office space. She came to understand the nature of the past and current building lease situations. She also talked with coworkers to learn about previous change initiatives—what worked and what didn't. Understanding the history of the office space configuration as well as previous change initiatives gave her insight to create an informed plan.

Why Initiate Change?

Initiate Change is an effective strategy for getting yourself engaged and being stimulated by your environment, your job, and new challenges. Perhaps it's time to step up and shake off your reputation for being passive. It's your opportunity to learn something new by getting involved. It's inspiring to make a difference instead of complaining about how things are. It's exciting to challenge yourself to solve a problem that has just cropped up or has long existed in your organization. At a personal level, identifying a specific change can help you develop new résumé-enhancing professional skills, such as how you identified an opportunity for improvement, gathered supporting data, created a plan, received management support, and helped implement the plan to success.

Besides what you get out of creating change, there's the benefit to the organization. Your improvements to the job, team, and/ or company will change the way others experience work. It may make their lives easier. There are many benefits to driving change in a positive direction. At a broader level, familiarizing your company with change can have strategic implications: a company's ability to evolve and respond to challenges will increase its ability to compete and succeed.

Is the Initiate Change Strategy Right for You?

The Initiate Change strategy reflects your desire to engage, challenge yourself to take on something new, and effectively bring it to resolution. This strategy is not for everyone. As much as experiencing change is a challenge, leading change is also not for the faint of heart. Use the following descriptions to determine whether this is the right strategy for you to create your end of work:

- *You're ready to move beyond complaints to action.* Are you tired of hearing yourself or others complain? Is it time to move beyond stating the obvious and take action? If you pride yourself on action (or would like to), this is the right strategy for you.

- *You long to apply your skills and talents to standing up for what you believe in and making a difference.* Do you know you have the ideas and skills to solve problems? Are you confident that your ideas are solid and well thought out, and you have the skills to make it happen? Then Initiate Change is the right strategy for you. You care about making things better for yourself and others around you. Get in there and make it happen.

- *You'd like to be more engaged with your work environment.* Are you the first to point out what's wrong with something—but the last one to actually do something about it? Perhaps you've been apathetic up to this point, but you realize that if there's anyone who could make something happen for the better, it's you! You've been looking for something to care about. You want to get more engaged and are tired of the way things are at work. It's time to get up off the couch and stand up for what you think is the right thing to do. Make a difference!

- *You have knowledge of the system that you could effectively use to change it for the better.* Do you believe that change can only happen from the inside? Sometimes, to make a difference, you must cross over to what you perceive as the "other side." There's nothing wrong with crossing over. Experiencing something from another's perspective can earn you credibility and effectively influence change. Having inside knowledge will help you initiate change appropriately and effectively.

If any of these four descriptions sound like you, use the Initiate Change strategy to help you create the end of work as you know it. This strategy will help you define what you want to improve and then do it.

Make Change a Reality

We've explored the Initiate Change strategy and why you might want to use it to create your end of work. Now that you've determined that the Initiate Change strategy is right for you, we will look at how to bring your Initiate Change strategy to life by figuring out what areas require change and how to effectively drive it.

DEFINE YOUR CHANGE

To effectively initiate change, you must be open to ideas for improvements, ask questions to understand the environment, choose which changes you want to be involved in bringing about, and then design and implement that change.

First, take a look around your world of work and create a list of the changes you want to make in your organization, whether it will affect just your projects or is something bigger. What are the things you find yourself or others complaining about? What's broken? What could be better? What would make your job or those of others easier? What would be the result if things were different?

When you take a look at your projects, what's not working so well? When you take a look at your team, what process could use improvement? When you take a look at your department, how could it function more effectively? When you take a look at your company, what would help it reach its target revenues and profit margins?

Next, you need to decide which opportunity (or opportunities) for improvement you want to take on as a challenge. Read through the list you've compiled. Which potential changes would make the biggest difference to people around you? Which of these are you genuinely interested in facilitating? The following criteria can help you determine which ones you want to drive:

1. What is the cost of driving this improvement? Do the benefits outweigh it? Can I make a business case for making an improvement?

2. Has this been attempted before? What were the lessons learned?

3. Who will be affected by this change? Do I have relationships and alliances with them, or can I create these?

4. Who needs to support or sponsor this initiative? My boss? Someone else? If appropriate or necessary, do I think I need an executive at the highest ranks to support this?

5. What will success look like? Is this realistic?

6. What is my motivation for taking on a given change?

After you have refined your list, based on these considerations, it's time to prioritize them. You can't realistically get to everything tomorrow, so which one—or ones—do you want to tackle first? Determine which you care about most and which will give you the greatest result for your effort.

YOUR INITIATE CHANGE ACTIONS

Now that you've chosen to make Initiate Change your strategy and have defined the changes you want to drive, we'll take a look at the attitudes and actions that will bring them to life. This section explores ways in which you can zoom in and out to shift your attitude and take actions to make your Initiate Change strategy a reality.

Zoom in and first consider the following principles. Your attitude influences your actions. Your actions create results that will support or hinder your change efforts. So to create the end of work as you know it, you must start with the right attitude.

When it comes to initiating change, attitude is everything. To keep you focused and help maintain your course if the going gets tough, let's zoom out to address the bigger picture. Here are four tips:

1. **Stay optimistic.** The Initiate Change strategy is about making something better. Your optimism for a better and brighter future is what drives your desire to do something. Share your optimism with coworkers and help them see this initiative positively too.

2. **Lead by doing.** Whether your road to improvements is easy or difficult, know that you're making a difference even by trying. You're demonstrating to others that you care enough about improvement to make the effort. Let that be an inspiration to coworkers to motivate themselves.

3. **Make a complete effort.** Engage in your change 100 percent. Change is tough. Give it your all, regardless of the speed bumps, politics, and naysayers. Even if you only move the change needle a little bit, you will know that you tried your best.

4. **Keep what is in it for *you* in mind**. What is your personal reward for your effort?

Once you are prepared with the right attitude to launch your change efforts, next comes the process of enlisting others for effective planning, design, and implementation of the change. So if, for instance, you've decided that you want to improve the current process for receiving orders from customers in order to get paid more quickly, you will have to enroll the support of the appropriate sales and finance leaders to effectively design a new order-taking process and plan for the implementation stage, which includes identification of the new system, configuration and customization of the system, training of the people affected, migration over to it from the old system, and communication about the entire process to everyone who's potentially affected. The key here is to take all possible elements into consideration in your planning and make it happen! Note: There are many change management models out there to guide you, especially on the Internet.

Take a look at the first change you want to drive. What is the business case for your change? Will it make money or reduce cost? After you've made the business case for it, you'll need to carefully create an action plan, which should address the following:

1. **Support for the change.** Who will be affected? Whose support do you need to enlist? Do they also need to be part of the planning of the change, or just put their name behind it?

2. **Design of the change.** Imagine the change successfully implemented. Keep the details of this goal in mind to inform you as you develop your design.

3. **Implementation of the change.** Plan for how you will implement the change. What will the communication process look like? What will be the milestones on the way to success?

4. **Evaluation of the change.** Establish criteria that will confirm whether the completed change meets your goals. What are some likely loose ends that you'll need to address?

The Initiate Change strategy can be simple or complex, depending on the level of impact on others. Know that change typically takes time and it's natural for others to go through a process of denial, resistance, exploration, and commitment.

Denial: "This can't be happening"

Resistance: "Maybe if I ignore it, it will go away" or "The way we do things now is better, and what you propose won't work here."

Exploration: "Hmm, I might be open to this if it will make my job easier."

Commitment: "I need to tell my team about this new process."

You will need to be prepared to walk coworkers through this process by empathizing with their experience and providing sufficient communication and support as recommended by Cynthia Scott in her 2004 book, *Managing Change at Work.*

You need to anticipate others' reactions to each stage of the change process and help them transition through it by acknowledging their concerns and highlighting the positive opportunity that it provides. This takes time. If you build your argument well, using both a strong business case and political savvy, you can help others come around. For example, this could mean knowing the behind-the-scenes people whose buy-in you *really* need to secure, because the figureheads will be taking their cue from them.

Initiating change is an exciting and stimulating strategy for creating your end of work. It calls on all of your skills of observation, analysis, planning, implementation, and relationship building. Initiating change demands your full engagement to see the opportunities and take action! It's a thrilling way to create your end of work.

3

DEMAND AUTONOMY

CASE STUDY

Although out of college for only five years, Stacy is a top performer and highly ranked by the people she manages at her Fortune 500 company. She is considered a maverick within a corporate culture that is viewed as conservative. Even though most of her peers are wary of deviating from the traditional company behavior, Stacy looks to take on risk because she can. She delivers such great results that she is free to blaze her own trail. However, the trail she blazes combines what she wants to achieve with the company's objectives. She is also clear on who she is, her strengths, and what she expects from her coworkers and company. Stacy succeeds at creating her own sense of autonomy within an environment that others consider stifling.

Have it your way! Clarity, individuality, and initiative are a few words to describe this strategy. Demand Autonomy when you want to draw your line in the sand to confirm your independence and personal goals, and take action to support your decisions.

Is This Strategy Right for You? Demand Autonomy if

- You want more freedom and control over your environment and destiny.
- You prefer to set your own pace so you can be your best.
- You like to move quickly to action.
- You get excited by challenging the bureaucracy and status quo.

When to Apply: At different points in your career, it's time to blaze a new trail. Demand Autonomy when you want to define your own boundaries and objectives and to make *what you want* happen for you. It is applicable for both everyday situations in which you need to banish ambiguity as well as to establish your longer-term goals. Demand Autonomy when it's time to get into the driver's seat.

What Autonomy Will Do for You: By using the Demand Autonomy strategy, you can define what you want, your span of control, and the actions you need to take. Moving down the autonomy path will require that you take stock of your strengths, level of office credibility, and opportunities to push your boundaries for growth and recognition.

Do you wake up in the morning and dread going to work because you have a boss who micromanages you? Could your work be more interesting if only you had the opportunity to work on projects that you were interested in and you could actually call the shots? If this sounds familiar, the strategy of demanding autonomy may be the right one for you. Demanding autonomy means you are through with the status quo and ready to break free from the bonds that hold you back from what interests and motivates you. Seek opportunities that motivate you and that will also produce positive results for your company.

What Is Autonomy?

Imagine a place you go to every day where you are able to bring out your best. In fact, you are asked for nothing but your best, and you are given the leeway to do what it takes to deliver. That's the end of work as you know it, and demanding autonomy will get you there.

Autonomy is your ability to fully express your ideas and do what it takes to turn those ideas into reality. Autonomy means you have the support of your coworkers, particularly your boss, to get the job done without being micromanaged. Demanding autonomy means that you are not afraid of challenging the status quo. Organizations often find themselves doing things a certain way because of preexisting patterns and history, not because it's the most effective way. Demanding autonomy calls you to challenge the bureaucracy inherent in organizations in a way that works for both you and your company.

Demand Autonomy as a strategy when you are clear on what you need to do at work to get your job done. Autonomy is also about taking control of your environment. The end of work as you know it comes about when you are able to do what you want to at work, isn't it? Demanding autonomy allows you to create what you want in your professional career.

Stacy, our autonomy expert, was clear that in order to get her job done and get stellar performance reviews at the end of the year, a bonus, and a promotion, she needed to take control of her destiny. Her company had been around for more than fifty years. Although still a leader in its market, its technology and its way of doing business were becoming close to obsolete. Stacy's choice: either go with the flow and be content with being just average or take on a new challenge, such as revamping the way the marketing team measures its success or repositioning her company's products for new, untapped markets. You can imagine which one she chose. But to blaze a new path while avoiding stepping on too many toes, Stacy knew she would need to get her boss's support.

Though autonomy has a great upside, demanding it can be a bit tricky. Like Stacy, you need the support of your boss. If you see an opportunity to take on a new project, bring your boss up to speed on the opportunity you see, the positives for the business, and benefits to personnel. Next, you need to understand the political environment in your organization. Identify any historical issues, players who have a stake in the status quo, and how new ideas have succeeded or failed in the past. If you have the support and understand the nuances, you can be effective at demanding autonomy and actually get things done—your way. Or maybe you just want to step up, speak up, and take an active role. But before stepping up, look around; know your environment and decide the most effective way to be more proactive.

The Principles of the Demand Autonomy Strategy

Two core principles define and drive autonomy. First, to justify your autonomy, you need to demonstrate your ability to *get things done*. Second, you need to *determine what you can control*. You may not be able to be autonomous in everything you do at work.

Here's a closer look at these two principles:

1. **Get things done.** If you like to talk about all the great things you will do in your project or job, but you don't follow through, you lose credibility. No one will grant you the autonomy you demand if you are a big talker—and only that. So get things done. Demonstrate that you are a person of your word. Let's face it; people who must be micromanaged aren't trusted to get things done. First build up your trust account. Without that, you can't demand anything.

When Stacy first started in her organization, she had very little credibility. She was fresh out of college with much to learn. She knew it would take time and consistent demonstration of results to earn autonomous status for herself. As her trust account grew slowly over time with her demonstrated excellence, she found ways to start to push the conventional boundaries of her job. She began with questions to understand how the company's system and bureaucracy had come to be. Instead of placing judgment on them, she strove to understand their history and context so she could more precisely find ways in which to push back on the system.

2. **Determine what you can control.** After you have demonstrated accountability for doing what you say you will do, assess your environment to more accurately determine what you can control. You may find there are certain projects in which you will not be able to be autonomous because of the individuals involved and the politics associated with them. You may have to bite your tongue and just go along for the ride. There's nothing wrong with choosing your battles—that's a key element of being politically savvy. As for the areas in which you determine that you can be autonomous and effective, this is where you can let loose. You have established the right relationships and earned the ability to do as you see fit for the organization. Use these areas to thrive in your autonomy.

As Stacy discovered ways in which to push back on the system, she got mixed results. Often her coworkers would tolerate and even actively support her maverick behaviors. They would be on her teams, support her projects, and in general act as advocates. But sometimes autonomy proved a challenge when it came to initiatives that had historic or political implications. After hitting a few bumps, Stacy started to look more closely at the individuals involved and the politics. More specifically, she started to understand what was important to them and why they were holding on to doing things in a particular way. Stacy decided to pick her battles carefully based on what she thought she could effectively control and influence. In her one-on-one meetings with her boss, Carrie, Stacy would share her observations and insights to help build her credibility with Carrie—who, by the way, was known for micromanaging. More important, the intent was to convey to Carrie that Stacy understood Carrie's concerns and so, over time, Carrie could trust her to make calls on the spot. This strategy paid off over time.

Why Demand Autonomy?

Demand Autonomy is your strategy for creating a space in which you influence your work environment, align what you want to achieve with the good of your company, and get to do things your way. Creating autonomy allows you a sense of independence and the ability to take charge in your workplace. Additionally, you want Demand Autonomy as a strategy to create more freedom in the context of your work. You're going to look at creatively redefining the existing boundaries such as your job expectations and workflow. Maybe you thought those boundaries were set in stone, so you never thought to challenge them. Whether your assumptions about testing boundaries and pushing the limits were informed by your personality or your upbringing, this may be your opportunity to break free of these confines. Now you can reexamine those assumptions to see where you can push for more freedom to do things your way.

Is the Demand Autonomy Strategy Right for You?

Your choice of this strategy is a reflection of a desire to take control over your work and have the freedom to do things as you see fit. Like all end of work strategies, this may or may not be right for you. Use the following descriptions to determine whether this is the right strategy for you to create your end of work:

- *You want more freedom and control over your environment and destiny.* Is it important to you to be able to do things your way? Particularly, do you want to be trusted to get the work done however and whenever you think it's best to do it? Do you think you should be evaluated based on your performance and not the number of hours you put into your job? You don't want to be stifled by a boss who insists that you are at your desk by 8 A.M. and wants a weekly itemized progress report.

- *You prefer to set your own pace so you can be your best.* Is the result more important than how you got to that result? Have you learned that you do your best work when collaborating with others over coffee? You don't want to be told that you should hurry up and get something done. You'd rather set your own pace and determine based on your observations of the environment which projects should be a priority, and when and how you will get to them.

- *You like to move quickly to action and do what needs to get done.* Do you love brainstorming and collaborating but understand that at the end of the day it's all about execution?

- *You get excited by challenging the bureaucracy and status quo.* Do you see that the way things have been done is not necessarily relevant and useful? Demand Autonomy is the right strategy for you if you can't stand that people see only one way in which to do something. You, however, see alternatives and are more than willing to take the calculated risk of trying a new way to get a better result. You don't apologize for trying something new.

If any of these four descriptions sound like you, use the Demand Autonomy strategy to help create the end of work as you know it. This strategy will help you define what you want to get done at work and how you want to go about doing it.

Make Autonomy a Reality

We've explored the definition of autonomy and why you would want to use this strategy to create your end of work. Now that you've determined that the Demand Autonomy strategy is the right one for you, we will explore how to bring it to life by determining the credibility you need to demonstrate and the areas you can control, then creating an action plan to make it a reality.

DEFINE YOUR AUTONOMY

To gain autonomy and remain autonomous, you must demonstrate that you can be trusted to do your job. The first step to defining your autonomy is to evaluate how much you have in your "trust account," that is, the level of trust and credibility you have established with your employer. On a scale of one to ten (ten being high), how much do you have in your account? Think back over the preceding year on the job. How did you rank in your last annual review? If you ranked in the middle or below, you will need to build credibility. How are you perceived by your coworkers and manager? Before you blaze your trail, you will want to make sure you have support. Are there any unresolved issues with your manager or coworkers? For example, perhaps you missed a deadline a few months back. Before launching your effort to establish autonomy, you need to rebuild your time management credibility.

Your level of trust and credibility with others also impacts how much control you have over your life at work and the decisions you can make. Do you feel like you are being micromanaged? Are you frustrated by the fact that you have limited room to make decisions? Is this inherent in your work role, or could your boss's controlling, anxious behavior be an inherent personality trait? If the former, you can focus on the next section. If it's the latter, however, then you need to take a closer look at this behavior. Even if it stems from her fundamental personality, does she behave this way with everyone on your team or just you? If she does this with everyone, then you need to provide gentle feedback that this is not working for you and you find it stifling your ability to get your work done. Make a request for *exactly* what you'd like to see done differently. For example, "Mary, I appreciate the attention to detailed directions you provide me. I've been doing this long enough that I don't need so many details. What I'm asking for is this: next time we discuss a project, if you could tell me what it is and what you want to see as an end result, I'd like the opportunity to figure out everything in between. Will that work for you?"

If you notice that this micromanaging behavior is directed at you and no one else on the team, your boss is expressing a lack of confidence in your work and the results. If you're new to the job, it's understandable that you will just need to prove yourself over time. If you're not so new, and it's about your performance, evaluate what you need to do better. Create a plan for how you'll make this happen. Identify projects you are currently working on, and define success for each of those projects. Identify the resources you will need to be successful. Are you lacking a skill set or discipline? Do you need additional training or help? Share this plan with your boss and get input and support. This will help you redefine your relationship with your boss so you can be more autonomous. Once you consistently demonstrate reliable, satisfactory work, then you can take a look at the areas in which you could be autonomous.

The second step to demanding your autonomy is to identify what you can control. Make a list of all the variables in your work environment: organizational culture, senior leaders, decision-making process, your boss, your coworkers, how everyone is being evaluated for performance and raises, your projects, and so on. Define the boundaries for each of them on a scale of one to ten (ten being most flexible). For instance, how much can you push the organizational culture to go from fear-based to inspirational? Perhaps two to five. How about moving your boss from micromanaging to letting go? Perhaps six to eight. Delineate how much you can control, then push the boundaries around a particular variable.

Put it all together. As you build your trust account and expand the areas you can control, what does autonomy look like for you? Does it mean that you go to work every day and exercise complete control over your projects? Specifically, can you affect the decisions about your project by influencing your peers? Perhaps you get to drive ideas for new projects as long as you make the time to come up with the projects. Create a description of what autonomy looks like in a typical day on the job. Revisit this twice a year or when you have a job change to determine whether it's still relevant.

YOUR DEMAND AUTONOMY ACTIONS

Now that you've chosen autonomy and have defined what it means to you to be autonomous, let's look at the attitude and actions that will bring this strategy to life. This application section explores ways in which you can zoom out to shift your attitude and zoom in to take actions to make your autonomy strategy a reality.

First consider the following general principles. Your attitude influences your actions. Your actions create results that will support or hinder your autonomy. So to create the end of work as you know it, you must start with the right attitude.

Here are three helpful attitude tips for the Demand Autonomy strategy:

1. **Think integrity.** Follow your instincts and do what you feel is right, despite what others may or may not be doing.

2. **Be proactive.** Seek opportunities. If there's something broken, take the initiative to fix it. Don't wait to be asked.

3. **Stay optimistic.** Depending on where you work, taking on a challenge, fixing something that is broken, or bettering yourself can be seen by others as a threat to the status quo. Keep your head and stay focused.

Where should you apply your newfound attitude? Pull out your description of what it means for you to be autonomous. How do these three attitudes affect the way you will go about expressing your autonomy? For example, if you want more freedom to work at your own pace and set your hours, will you be willing to stay later or come in earlier if something comes up and it's the right thing to do?

Also, what resources are needed to make your autonomy a reality? These may include staff support, time, and maybe even allocation of funds. They could include support from your boss when you see something is broken and you want to take the initiative to drive a solution from concept to reality. Or it could be your boss's giving you the freedom to do your projects as long as you deliver on time and with quality.

To bring your autonomy into reality may also mean you have to find the strength and confidence to ask for what you really need without feeling guilty. How is autonomy framed in your mind? Is it a luxury or something you need? If demanding autonomy is your strategy to achieve your end of work, it's not a luxury. It's something you need. It's time to step up and demand it.

Now, demanding autonomy generally means not really *demanding*, but rather *asking* for autonomy. As with any effective request, consider your audience: what's in it for them? Barging into your boss's office, slamming down your fist, and demanding autonomy will probably not only fail to get you autonomy but also might get you a security escort to the parking lot. A request and a plan, however, can take you a long way. Frame your request in a way that presents your thought process, reasoning, and, most important, the benefit for your boss and the company. Start with your successes and contributions, then build on how you take initiative.

You'll boost your chances of getting your boss's buy-in if you have demonstrated your ability to work without supervision and how having that space has helped you deliver results.

Demand Autonomy is your ideal strategy if you are inspired to take initiative, lead, and take control of your environment. The tension of having to go to work to fulfill the objectives of someone or something else can be stifling. Choosing autonomy can be a powerful method for realizing your goals and at the same time helping your company achieve its objectives.

4

CREATE MEANING

Sam is a software engineer. With ten years in the profession and three years at his current company, Sam had come to the point of feeling hungry for something new. But what's next? Work was getting boring; same routines, projects, and the same obstacles. At a deeper level, Sam's job lacked a connection with his growing desire to make a difference in the world. Back in college, Sam had studied and volunteered for the causes he was passionate about: weekends helping to feed poor city residents, summers traveling abroad to teach in impoverished villages. He had not anticipated that he would ever find himself in a job that was not directly connected to the causes he believed in. He wants to contribute to something that is consistent with his beliefs in helping others and could affect people in his community. What if he quit his job and went to work for a nonprofit? But the idea of bailing on his company and taking a substantial hit to his salary seemed too extreme.

Sam took a second look at the opportunities within his company and decided to lead the effort to create a community outreach group on behalf of his company. The group's goals were to address needs in the community and highlight the causes that his company supported. This endeavor enabled Sam to create something that had social impact and fulfilled his desire to be with a company that matched his values.

Stop talking about what's important and what you stand for. Do it. Create Meaning when it's time to connect your job, efforts, and time to something beyond yourself. Redefine the context of what you do to see how your job positively affects the world. The workplace takes on a different dimension and presents new opportunities when you are clear on how your efforts can make a difference outside the walls of your company.

Is This Strategy Right for You? Create Meaning if

- You want to bring all of who you are to your job.

- You work for a company and with people who care about the larger community.

- You are driven to connect your work to worthy causes to make an impact.

- You want to redefine the context of your job to create and implement your ideals.

When to Apply: Create Meaning when you need your job to have significance, want a connection to something larger, and want to use your job as a vehicle to support what is important to you.

What Creating Meaning Will Do for You: By using the Create Meaning strategy, your work can take on a larger significance and be a reflection of your values. Taking the path of meaning will require that you get clear on what's most important to you and find ways to create that in your current work.

Aside from the Jane Goodalls of the world, most of us struggle to find meaning in the work we do. For instance, how does creating a PowerPoint presentation on this quarter's revenues or sitting through another day full of meetings make a difference in the world? Even if you're employed at a nonprofit that's working to create change, do you feel like your daily task of answering hundreds of emails really has an impact? If you are the type of person who struggles to discover how your work and everyday life positively affect people and the world, then Create Meaning could well be the right strategy for you to use to create the end of work as you know it.

What Is Meaning?

Imagine waking up every morning and feeling energized by your restful night's sleep. You slept deeply because your mind was quiet. Despite all the madness in the world, you know that you do your best to make a difference. Although you have not ended world hunger, you take every step that one person can possibly take. Why? Because you have a good job that pays the bills *and* also allows you to act on the larger ideas you hold important to your work. That's work that has meaning.

Meaning enables you to go to work every day and feel like it's a place where you can make your values a reality. What are these values? They can be anything that is important to you. It doesn't necessarily have to be something as dramatic as saving lives, but it has to be something that is significant to you. If you have a love of music, then your work has meaning when it supports you in expressing your musical talents, learning more about music, being around musicians, or affecting the music industry. You don't have to dodge whalers' harpoons on the deck of a Greenpeace boat to feel like you are making a difference.

Use Create Meaning as a strategy when you are clear on what you really care about and that you want to use your work as a means to fulfill this. Most of us assume that work must be in service of our employer's needs. But you can also make work serve your need to have meaning in your life and use work as an outlet for manifesting what's important to you.

For Sam, our resident meaning expert, the immediate community around which his company operated was important to him. He always felt that, although the company served the community by creating jobs, it didn't really do anything further for the community. Sam is the type of person who thinks it's important to give to others and be generous. He didn't realize—until he had worked for the company for a few years and he started seeing how the community needed help with certain events—just how important this was to him. For instance, during annual food drives the people in the community stepped up, but his company never took the initiative to sponsor events, make substantial food donations, or support employees who took time off work to volunteer. He realized how important it was to help those in need and that there were many opportunities for the company to show goodwill toward the community. The light bulb went on, and Sam understood how he could make his work more meaningful. He could raise awareness within his company of the abundant opportunities to give and at the same time raise awareness of his company's contribution in the larger community. Suddenly work became a place where he could make a difference.

This particular definition of meaning is not a judgment placed on what is valuable and important to you. Rather, it is based on making a conscious decision about what is important to you and finding a way to bring that into your work. When you see your workplace as an outlet for pursuing what's important to you, you can see your work as a place of opportunity. Those long drawn-out meetings and PowerPoint presentations become a vehicle for something larger, because they fit into what you want to achieve.

The Principles of the Create Meaning Strategy

Two major principles form the basis of meaning: *values* and *connections*. First, define what you consider important and what you value. Then look for the connections between your values and what you do. These principles form the basis of how to achieve the meaning you desire to create your end of work.

Here's a deeper dive into the two principles.

1. Values. What do I hold most important to me?

Your values and what you hold as important may change over time with the events in your life. As a single person, you may have held your friendships important to you—sometimes even more important to you than your dysfunctional family. As the tides change and you marry and have children, that value may shift to the importance you place on your new family.

There were a number of things that Sam held important, including meaningful relationships with people—among them family, friends, and his local community. Not only did he see himself as a social creature who thrived on having meaningful relationships with people, but he also felt that through investing in those relationships much was always given back to him. So when he saw his company's lack of connection to the community, he felt uncomfortable, but he wasn't sure it was his place to do anything about it.

2. **Connections.** What is the relationship between my values and my work?

Now that you've defined your values, to create your end of work you must look for how your values are connected to your work. How are they aligned? If they are not, is there any way for you to align them? Here is an opportunity to get creative. When you can bring the two into harmony and create a connection, you can make your work a place to express your values. How great is that?

When Sam noticed that his values of being a part of and contributing to his community were not expressed in the workplace, he felt that something was off. Sure, he had strong relationships with coworkers, but there was virtually no relationship between his company and the greater community. Over time, this began to really bother him. When he realized that what he held near and dear to his heart was the idea of creating stronger relationships, he also realized work could be an outlet for expressing what was important to him. The connection became clear. It was no longer just a discomfort, but a clear disconnect between his values and his work. Something had to be done. That's when he took action to create a community outreach program. Of course, he had to go through all the right channels, but the energy and momentum behind his efforts were fueled by the desire to create meaning at the workplace.

Why Create Meaning?

Create Meaning is your strategy for creating alignment between what is important to you and what you do for a living. If you desire to make a difference in the world or connect your effort to something larger, then the Create Meaning strategy can help you find a way to bring about that alignment. Imagine no longer wandering around aimlessly, wondering why you even took the job in the first place, but instead establishing your work as a place for making a difference in programs and causes you consider important.

Additionally, you may well want to Create Meaning if you have never stopped to really think about what's important to you. Many of us go through life in such a rush to get here and there, to get things done, or just to get to the end of the day that we don't stop to think about how any of that connects to something deep and important to us. Create Meaning if you want to take the opportunity to ponder this very important question, "What exactly do I hold important to me?"

Is the Create Meaning Strategy Right for You?

Use the following descriptions to determine whether this is the right strategy for you to create your end of work:

- *You want to bring all of who you are to your job.* Have you ever thought it best to keep certain things about yourself, to yourself? And we don't mean the socially and professionally inappropriate stuff. We're talking about the things you believe in. Isn't it frustrating to have to leave all that at home when you go to work? No wonder so many of us are so disengaged with our jobs. Maybe you've come to accept that you should simply show up, do your job, and collect your paycheck. But you do have a choice: work can be either void of meaning or a conduit for what you believe in. The Create Meaning strategy is your opportunity to focus on your values and how they shape and influence your contribution.

- *You work for a company and with people who care about the larger community.* Do you truly care about what your company stands for and how it's making a difference in the world? Then Create Meaning is your strategy for how to create your end of work. It's important to you that you work for a company that you can proudly stand behind. Its efforts are making a positive impact in the world. Yes, you may have disagreements on how to go about delivering on your company's promise, but you agree on the big picture and the ethical standards by which your company operates.

- *You are driven to connect your work to greater causes to make an impact.* Perhaps your company is not making a direct difference in the social causes you care about. However, you know you are making an incremental difference with your on-the-job habits, behaviors, and perspective. Although you are driven by the desire to make a difference in the world in which you live, you know you can't stop world hunger tomorrow. You are realistic. You take slow and measured steps to ensure that every ounce of effort counts toward something. For example, in your procurement role, you ensure that company suppliers are green-certified, practice and promote recycling, and have a neutral carbon output. Whether your job has a direct or indirect effect on the well-being of others, you get up every morning and go to work because you care and know that you can make a difference, whether it's big or small. You live your life with no regrets because you are clear on how your work is connected to a greater cause, and you are helping the world improve, slowly but surely.

- *You want to redefine the context of your job to create and implement your ideals.* Are you clear that your work needs to have a deeper meaning, but you don't know quite how to get there? You know what's important to you, and you are looking for ways to bring this to your work. You realize it's the only way for you to truly get excited about what you're doing day to day. Volunteering in your spare time is not enough. You know your company can make a bigger impact just by its sheer size. You are looking for ways to make that happen. You are even willing to devote your personal time to this effort, and you need to find a way to leverage your company's name and presence.

If any of these four descriptions reflect you or what you are looking for, use the Create Meaning strategy to help you create the end of work as you know it. Your Create Meaning strategy will help you confirm your values and create connections to make the things that are important to you an everyday part of your life.

Make Meaning a Reality

We've explored the definition and underlying principles of the Create Meaning strategy. Now that you've determined that this strategy is the right one for you to use to create the end of work as you know it, we will explore how to bring your Create Meaning strategy to life by first confirming your values and their connection to your work and then creating an action plan to make your meaning a reality.

DEFINE YOUR MEANING

Use this section to define what's important to you and the meaning you will create as part of your job.

Take this opportunity to zoom out—to take a step back and reflect on what's important to you in your life. When push comes to shove, what do you care most about? If you were to choose a social cause, what would that cause or organization be? What principles or values do you hold as the most important? As you take a look at your answers, what themes pop out? In Sam's example, the broad focus is his desire to make a difference in his community—specifically, banishing hunger. As you zoom out and take a look at your list, what are the bigger themes you see emerging? Is it that you care about making things right in the world and that things need to be fair and just? Do you see the world as a place to learn and grow? Do you see the world through the lens of excitement and new experiences? Or is the act of accomplishing something of significance—making an impression, leaving a legacy—more important to you? You may find that a number of themes are important to you.

Now that you've identified what's important to you, let's take a look at how it can be connected to your work. Sam saw that his workplace could also be a place to help his community. What's the connection for you? Be creative, and don't censor your ideas. If it is important to you to help the environment, is there a way for you to integrate these beliefs into your projects, job, or company? For example, there may be an opportunity to introduce new recycling practices that will save the company money and create less waste. Realistically, not every job can be linked to a significant cause on a global or national scale. But there's still a way to create affinity groups—to get together with like-minded colleagues, brainstorm, and put your values to work. Take a look your themes and imagine ways to align your values to your work and create more meaning in what you do.

YOUR CREATE MEANING ACTIONS

Now that you've chosen to make Create Meaning your strategy and found a way to link it to your work, it's time to make it a reality. Let's look at the attitude and actions that will bring them to life. This application section explores ways in which you can zoom in and out to shift your attitude and take actions to make your meaning a reality.

Here are three helpful attitude tips:

1. **Be yourself.** You are clear on who you are and what's important to you. You live your life with intentionality and purpose.

2. **Be optimistic.** You have to believe that there's more to life and this world than simply what you are working on today. Imagine the possibilities! Your optimism is your guide, even in times of doubt when others question you and put you down.

3. **Be proactive.** You are more than just talk. You don't just wait around for things to happen. You turn your ideas into actions.

Where should you apply your newfound focus? Pull out your list of themes and the links to your work. How do these three attitudes affect the way you will go about expressing your meaning? In the face of people challenging your ideas, remember to be yourself and stand up for your beliefs, see the possibilities even within the challenges, and above all, make it happen. Don't give others a reason to say, "It's another great idea, but who's going to do it, and when will you or they find the time?"

First, what will you need to successfully initiate and complete projects, actions, and activities that support your meaning? What resources are needed? These may include staff support, time, and perhaps a budget. For instance, if reducing your carbon footprint is important to you and you want to bring this value and practice to your organization, you will need help to do the research, analysis, and recommendations. This includes staff support to analyze your company's current practices, how it impacts the environment and what it costs the company, and budget for solutions implementation.

Second, to whom do you need to communicate your ideas around creating meaning? The people around you can play an important role in helping you achieve your meaning. These important people would most likely include your boss and closest colleagues.

Third, what requests do you need to make of your colleagues to get their support—not just their commitment to provide resources, but also mental support to help you think through roadblocks and emotional support to cheer you on? It's critical to enlist supporters to help cheer you on when you run into difficulties or people who just don't understand what you are trying to do.

To bring your meaning forward into reality may put more work on your plate, but if it's important to you, you're likely to find yourself willing and able to put in the extra time and effort— and the results will be well worth it. You may also be recognized by your colleagues and company when performance review time comes and you are able to show how you've gone above and beyond the call of duty, taking the initiative to do something that positively affects the world beyond your company. After all, at most companies, just doing your job gets you a satisfactory rating. But when you do a great job in your current responsibilities *and* take initiative to go above and beyond that, you can expect an excellent rating. Not only will you be satisfying the requirements of your job, but you also, by getting more from your experience at work, will create your end of work.

Create Meaning to get clear on what's important to you, take action, and make a difference. People who choose to create meaning focus on making their workplace a conduit for their values and for helping the causes they believe in. Whether to make a difference in their community or to help to change the world, people who choose the Create Meaning strategy are ready to bring what is important to them to what they do for a living.

5

SPARK
CREATIVITY

Musician, artist, and actor—so what is Tony doing as an IT project manager? He balances his love for technology with a hard-wired need to create. Tony is able to satiate his creative side on the job by offering different ways of designing a project or implementing a technical solution. When things get too linear and predictable, he looks at his work environment as an opportunity for creativity and innovation. As a result, he often finds himself invited into other groups' projects to help work through impasses or brainstorm new solutions. He loves bringing his creative side to his profession.

Paint the corporate canvas. Spark Creativity to make your job and company an outlet for your creative side. Bring new ideas, embrace curiosity, and allow yourself to innovate. Apply your personal interests and insights to solve problems in your workplace and generate innovative solutions. Experience your job environment through creative eyes to see new opportunities, renew your enthusiasm, and recharge for the long haul.

Is This Strategy Right for You? Spark Creativity if

- You want to bring your creativity and new ideas to your job.

- You are motivated to push the envelope and create something revolutionary.

- You see possibilities and opportunities and want to inspire others to do the same.

- You are ready to view your current projects, role, and work in a new and exciting way.

When to Apply: Many work environments are a palette of gray: draining, monochromatic, and dull. Get more from your work. Bring color, new ideas, and inspiration. Spark Creativity when it's time to breathe life into your work and expand the boundaries of what is possible. It's time to view your workplace and projects in a completely new light.

What Creativity Will Do for You: Spark Creativity to give yourself an emotional boost, see your workplace from a new perspective, apply the insights from your personal interests, and inspire yourself to seek opportunities. Embracing your creative side will open the door to make your job more engaging, challenging, and fun.

Was the workplace intended to be bland and monotonous? At what point in our careers did we accept that work must stifle our creative side? Why can't creativity be an integral part of what you bring to the table? If you believe that you should express your vitality and creative energy at work as well as in your personal life, consider what sparking creativity in your work life could do for you.

What Is Creativity?

Imagine coming to work every day and instead of just being asked to do your best at the usual tasks, being asked to challenge common thinking, test the way things are done, and discover new methods for solving problems or creating new ideas. These days lots of lip service is given to the concept of innovation, but for those who truly step up to the plate and see their work as a creative outlet, innovation is not a luxury, but an integral part of their experience of work. Looking at your workplace through the lens of creativity is a choice you make to bring forth your creative side. It feels good to contribute and create something that wasn't there before or share a perspective that influences others. That's the magic of the Spark Creativity strategy to end work as you know it.

No matter what your job or profession is, creativity involves giving your ideas the chance to come alive. You do this by challenging yourself to look at problems from a different angle. You make use of your insights from areas of interest outside of work. You apply solutions from one context to a new one. This allows you to look for ways to do things differently and be willing to throw your ideas out there to be challenged, trusting that even if some are turned down, even better ones will arise and ultimately win support. You have no ego and attachment to your ideas. You just want to see the best of them come to life and make a positive difference.

Spark Creativity as a strategy when you are tired of holding back your ideas or want to push yourself to become more engaged and inspired. Take the risk that your new ideas may not be accepted all of the time. What does it matter that they are unconventional or even quirky? When you can get over yourself or your concern that your ideas could be rejected, you can fully bring all your ideas to light for further scrutiny, exploration, and refinement. That's the only way for creativity to turn into innovation for your organization—and that's a fulfilling contribution to make. If an idea is rejected, first seek to understand whether a component of the idea is being rejected or its entirety. Second, separate your idea from yourself: it's not about you. Yes, this can be a challenge—after all, it's your idea. However, when you choose creativity, you're choosing to see things in a new way and to share your perspective. Your coworkers haven't asked for this change, and they may not be ready for a new way of thinking.

Consider our creativity expert, Tony. He hadn't always brought his creativity to bear on his work. He started the job just trying to be the corporate guy, coming in to solve problems by the book. This was a relatively new company, but with established ways of doing things. Tony didn't want to stir things up too soon. However, it wasn't long before he felt stifled. Although his solutions were effective, he wanted to take more risks and push the status quo with fresh thinking and new ideas. Tony sat down with his manager to discuss how he was feeling, his ideas, and what he saw as opportunities to contribute his creativity. His manager liked his ideas and even let Tony know that Tony's creativity and problem-solving skills were some of the main reasons he had wanted Tony to join the company in the first place. With that encouragement, Tony quickly got over his inhibitions and opened the floodgates. The ideas starting rolling. Not only were they good ideas, but Tony started feeling engaged. He felt energized that he didn't have to hold back his ideas or pass up perceived opportunities to make something even better. His risk-taking and creativity in turn influenced others to take risks, share ideas, and create a trusting environment for collaboration.

The Principles of the Spark Creativity Strategy

In each of us, ideas, innovation, and creativity spring from different sources. No matter where you draw your creative inspiration from, these three principles can help structure and guide your creative processes.

1. **Permission.** Make the space for creativity by first allowing yourself to be creative.

Most people working in traditional office environments have concerns and inhibitions about being seen as too far out or extreme. You may not want to admit it, but the herd mentality, although not sexy, is safe. You need to realize that you can still play it safe as you bring your creativity to the table. The first step is granting yourself permission to open up your work to your creative side. This begins with a simple question of "What if?" "What if we tried this a different way?" "What if I did . . . ?"

During his initial period of dissatisfaction, Tony needed to reflect on his current contribution to realize that he wasn't allowing himself the opportunity to be creative and thrive. He posed the question: what if I removed my inhibitions about contributing my creativity?

2. **Multidisciplinary approach.** Draw from any and every applicable source.

Draw from your experiences. Expand your interests. The more experiences you have and the more exposure to different things, the more sources of ideas and creative options you have to draw on. When you draw from your different experiences and interests in life, you create more potential for your ideas. Why not make use of the experiences you've had throughout your life? Bring the lessons you've learned to your workplace. Apply them to your work and see what new solutions you generate. Your beer-brewing hobby can benefit your chemistry research. Your video production experience lends itself to project management. Perhaps your experience as a preschool teacher is perfect for your new role as a manager.

Tony had pursued many interests over the years on his own time. He plays the sax, and from time to time he would perform at local venues with his buddies. He took some acting classes and thought he would challenge himself to try out for a small-budget play at the community theater. He had fun pursuing these interests because it allowed him to explore and develop a different side of himself. He never thought to pursue any of this professionally because he wanted to make more money and have a steady pay-check. When Tony decided to spark his creativity at work, he looked at problems through multiple lenses. He drew from his live performance experience to develop a communication strategy for deploying his company's new global technology standards.

3. Risk-taking. Know that not every idea will be embraced.

A big part of being creative on the job is knowing that not every idea or innovative solution will be embraced—and they probably shouldn't be either. The power of sharing your creativity is not always in the adoption of your ideas; rather, it's in stimulating and offering your ideas for consideration as a starting point. A key part of this strategy is being open to letting ideas flow quickly and creatively. But this means that not all ideas will hit the target, and that's OK. Sharing your ideas requires accepting that people may not understand them or be open to integrating them into their work. Be prepared with this mind-set. An open perspective will help you articulate your ideas in a way that demonstrates your openness and flexibility.

For Tony, taking the risks to share his ideas, no matter how far out they might have been, and letting go of needing them to be adopted was part of his resolution to no longer hold back. To be completely engaged and honest with himself, he needed to take the risk of being completely forthright with his colleagues. The result of his risk-taking was open communication, richer ideas, and a reaffirmed commitment to his work.

Why Spark Creativity?

Are you tired of being bored at work? Creativity is your outlet for bringing fun, excitement, and renewed energy to your daily routine. You deserve to go to work every day with the possibility of coming up with something new. There will always be problems to solve at work. You can look at those problems as either another obstacle you have to address or an opportunity for you to unleash your creativity.

There's a fringe benefit to sparking creativity. Ultimately, you end up inspiring others around you to do the same. It takes just one person to try something new to create a snowball effect. You could be *that* person. Wouldn't it be great to inspire your coworkers to follow in your footsteps and spark their own creativity? Imagine how innovative your organization can become when you and your coworkers can freely brainstorm ideas for new solutions without hesitation—and without egos getting in the way.

Is the Spark Creativity Strategy Right for You?

Creativity is a reflection of you as a complex individual with many interests and experiences. Your ability to bring this entire person to work can bring about the end of work as you know it. Review the following descriptions to determine whether this is the right strategy for you:

- *You want to bring your creativity and new ideas to your job.* If you feel that you've left a big part of yourself at home all these years, then it's time to make the leap. Spark Creativity and bring your novel ideas to work. It's time to make yourself whole and your work more complete. You can't afford to waste another day suppressing yourself. Make Spark Creativity your strategy for generating the experience of work as something that excites you. Give yourself permission to bring your ideas to the table to create the best solutions possible.

- *You are motivated to push the envelope and create something revolutionary.* If you like to push boundaries and see how far you can run with an idea or how outrageous you can get, this strategy is a good match for you. This is your opportunity to create revolutionary new ideas, not evolutionary ideas. It's the only way to truly break the mold and do something that will make a monumental difference.

- *You see possibilities and opportunities and want to inspire others to do the same.* If you have brought creativity to your work all these years, but haven't exactly managed to inspire others to do the same, then now it's time for a fresh effort. Be explicit about what you are doing to generate creative solutions. Encourage others to do the same, especially when you know that their ideas could be better than yours and may result in an even greater solution. Coach them through a problem instead of giving them your answers. Help them think through solutions, then ask more questions from different angles to further explore their ideas. Sparking creativity is your way to give back to others and inspire them to greater heights.

- *You are ready to view your current projects, role, and work in a new and exciting way.* If you need to refresh your outlook on work, then this could be the right strategy for you. You've tried it all—taken the motivational seminars, received feedback and coaching, and even created a development plan for yourself. But have you tried the creativity route? Have you challenged yourself to see your projects, role, and work through the lens of multidisciplinary possibilities and solutions? Take this opportunity to try out a new strategy that means bringing your whole self to work. Bring your guitar along and leave it in your cubicle to remind yourself that you are more than just an accountant—you are a musician, a parent, and many other things. All this makes you unique and uniquely qualified to contribute your ideas.

If any of these four descriptions resonate, you are a likely candidate for using the Spark Creativity strategy to help you create the end of work as you know it. The Spark Creativity strategy will help you give yourself the space to be creative and encourage you to look at the world of work through all the lenses that make you a unique individual.

Make Creativity a Reality

We've explored the definition and underlying principles of creativity. Now that you've determined that the Spark Creativity strategy is one you want to try to create the end of work as you know it, we will explore how to bring this strategy to life by first defining what creativity will look like for you and then creating an action plan to make it a reality.

DEFINE YOUR CREATIVITY

Tony's performance wake-up call prompted him to bring creativity into his work. When he gave himself the permission and space to bring more innovative solutions to the table, he saw his projects in a different light. He earned the reputation of being a creative problem solver, but not without thoughtfulness and hard work.

Use this section to define what creativity looks like for you and what you will need to do make it a reality. First, get real. How have you been holding back on your creativity, whether it's little or big time? For instance, do you second-guess yourself when you come up with a new idea every now and then? Or worse yet, do you not even allow yourself to go there at all? When it comes to brainstorming time, do you find yourself frozen from the pressure of having to come up with *something—anything*? Whether we are naturally creative or find it difficult to be creative, we all have those negative, fearful voices in our heads that can hold us back and stop us before we even try.

What's holding you back? Is it your self-talk, that you never thought about it, or that you didn't want to care until now? Give yourself permission to be creative. Now, this will mean something very different for each person. It could mean that from now on you won't hesitate to share your ideas, even if you think others may judge them as outrageous. Or it could mean that from now on you will remind yourself that being creative is not pressuring yourself, but turning yourself loose. Or it could mean setting yourself a goal, challenging yourself to be more creative. You'll need to figure out for yourself what this "permission to be creative" looks like for *you*.

Second, inventory the areas of discipline in which you have experience or expertise. Do you play a particular sport? If you don't play sports, what form of exercise do you like? What artistic endeavors do you like? Do you play a musical instrument, or do you particularly enjoy a certain type of music? What other content areas are you interested in? Do you have a love for good food and wine? Are you familiar with the fermentation process for home-brewed beer?

Once you've identified your areas of interest, experience, and expertise, categorize them and look for ways in which they influence your worldview and can be brought to bear on your projects and work. For instance, you love food and wine, and you are an avid cook. You love to use existing recipes as a starting point to create your own dishes. Back on the job, how can you use your creative mind for adapting existing "recipes" to solve problems and look at situations in a new light? That yearly audit that always takes too much time because the process is outdated is a great candidate for your creative recipe-enhancing skills.

There are many facets to each of us as an individual. That's what makes each of us unique—and uniquely qualified to be creative in a way no other person can be. Each person can generate a unique set of solutions with a particular set of interests and gifts.

You've made significant investments in those outside areas that interest you. Leverage those investments by using them as analogies to problems you encounter in the workplace. You'll find that the problems you've been able to solve in the areas that interest you most are also applicable to the workplace. Bring all of who you are and watch yourself flourish.

YOUR SPARK CREATIVITY ACTIONS

Now that you've chosen to make Spark Creativity your strategy, defined what being creative means to you, and given yourself permission to be creative and use your personal interests as a lens through which to solve problems, it's time to put it all into action.

Here are three helpful attitude tips:

1. **Be confident.** Don't feel shy about coming to the table with an idea. You don't need to apologize for thinking, particularly for thinking beyond the way things have always been done. If someone judges your idea as unworkable, let them know you are at least trying to generate all possible ideas.

2. **Be curious.** Give each idea some merit. Stay in curiosity mode. Instead of exploring why the idea won't work, explore it from the angle of what it would look like if it did work. You may be surprised at the solutions you come to, and it is a lot more exciting to be in a conversation about how to make something work.

3. **Encourage collaboration.** Although you may determine in the exploration process that an idea won't work, it can spark another one. Innovation also comes from building off of other people's ideas. Some of the best work has come out of this iterative process.

Where should you apply your newfound attitude? Create a list of all the problems you are currently experiencing in the following four categories: your project, role, department, and organization. That might be quite a lengthy list. Prioritize the problems within each of the four categories. Let's start with the number one priority on your project list, as this likely affects you most immediately.

Given that you are giving yourself the space to be creative, maintaining the right attitude, and bringing your unique multi-disciplinary viewpoint to bear, what solutions do you see to your current problem? Take a moment to reflect on this. Share your ideas with a trusted coworker and see if you can't come up with a solution you hadn't considered before. As with any new idea or solution, make sure you look at it from the perspective of all the key stakeholders and how they might be affected by this new solution. Is it truly a gain for everyone? If so, it may be an easier sell. If it requires a compromise, be prepared for some push back and negotiations. Address the concerns of your audience and detail the benefits of your approach. Invite their questions and suggestions, and work with them *creatively* to reach common ground. Now go through the remaining problems on your list. What new solutions are you generating? Notice how your new angle and new tools bring a renewed sense of optimism and energy to your work.

Don't get discouraged if your first creative solution doesn't take off. You might need to put a couple of them out there before one gets accepted. Whether or not you get your way is not necessarily the point (although it would be a nice win and certainly positive reinforcement). The real point is that you are creating your end of work by integrating your creative side into something that would otherwise not be as exciting and enjoyable for you.

Spark Creativity in your work to integrate the enjoyable and exciting parts of your life that currently exist only outside of work. You'll find that this not only brings refreshed energy and a different perspective to your job, but also gives you the opportunity to see problems in a new light. Now you can come up with solutions that normally would be applied in one situation and apply them in a different context. Many organizations talk about encouraging their employees to think "outside the box," but most of us have no clue what that *really* means. We understand we are being asked to be more creative—which is a great goal to set for ourselves—but we haven't known just how to go about it, until now. Spark Creativity by allowing yourself the space to be creative and apply your insights to the place in your life where you've never applied (or have been reluctant to apply) them before: the place where you work. Welcome to your end of work.

6

SEIZE
RECOGNITION

CASE STUDY

Diane has worked for the same rapidly growing company for almost three years. In concurrence with the company's growth, she has held a number of different positions. These moves have kept her interested in her job. However, over the last six months she has felt that maybe it was time to search for not just a new position but an entirely new company. She has felt increasingly bored and unappreciated. Serendipitously, Diane was tapped to create the company's disaster recovery strategy. Disaster recovery was something she knew absolutely nothing about, but it is tremendously important to the survival of any company if it ever faces a calamity. Beyond the intellectual and logistical challenges, Diane saw this project as an opportunity to gain recognition as the person who could help the company overcome any significant event.

Take a bow. Toiling for days, let alone years, in silent anonymity gets old. You deserve to be acknowledged. Recognition will confirm your contributions and strengths and validate your efforts.

Is This Strategy Right for You? Seize Recognition if

- You are ready to speak up after being quiet and under the radar.

- You deserve acknowledgment for who you are and what you've done.

- You desire to achieve status (that is to say, become a top contributor or climb the corporate ladder) or just receive acknowledgment from the CEO.

- You want something in return for your efforts.

When to Apply: Seize Recognition because others need to be aware of how much you have to offer—and have already accomplished. You have contributed to the company and made a difference. It's time to make sure you receive the accolades you deserve on a regular basis from peers, your manager, and your family.

What Recognition Will Do for You: Aside from securing that promotion, Seize Recognition to define the traits, skills, and knowledge that make you stand out. Your hard work has gone unrecognized for far too long because you haven't taken the time to ensure that others realize your contributions.

Do you walk down the hallways at work and wonder, "If I were to quit today, would anyone notice?" OK, so maybe your boss would notice, but would anyone else? Have you done so little to contribute to the company that people haven't even noticed? More than likely, you've done some outstanding work but never got credit for it. If the latter is the case, you aren't alone. Every day, millions of people go unrecognized for their hard work and effort. Your accomplishments have gone unsung not just because other people are too self-absorbed to notice; more than likely, you haven't taken the time to let others know. Now is your time to shine. Seize Recognition as your strategy to create the end of work as you know it.

What Is Recognition?

Imagine going to work every day and being thanked for all the big and little things you do. How would that change your experience of work? You might actually feel like you are making a difference and that, regardless of the size of your paycheck, it's enough that the people around you notice and appreciate your contributions. Welcome to the Seize Recognition strategy.

Seizing recognition means taking action to not only receive, but to seize, the accolades that belong to you. The human desire for recognition is fundamental: "Recognize me for my efforts and I will continue to gladly produce." It's positive reinforcement in action. You have been toiling in silence (perhaps for many years) hoping to be thanked for your work. That time has passed, and the dawn of seizing recognition is here to end work as you know it.

Seize Recognition is the ideal strategy when you are tired of sitting around and waiting for others to say "Thank you." The key is to be active, not passive. To *receive* recognition is passive. It means you are relying on others to notice and then actually make the effort to say something. Given the frenzied pace of life and work today, it's understandable that most people don't make the time to thank others for their contributions in the workplace. So why passively rely on others for your positive reinforcement? Be proactive. Seize it. Communicate your contributions, how you make a difference, the praise you receive from a happy client, and the problems that you solve. Let others know not just about your contribution but how they can learn and borrow from your successes.

Our recognition expert, Diane, had not previously seized recognition. She was bored at her job and feeling unappreciated. Regardless of how great or little her contributions, she never got recognized. It was as if she was never there. Her wake-up call was seeing the opportunity to do something new that would receive company-wide attention, and realizing that although she got lucky that an opportunity presented itself, she couldn't rely on that always happening. Instead of waiting for things to happen, she needed to take the initiative to step into the spotlight, make a difference, and share her success.

To Seize Recognition can feel awkward. If you are not used to calling attention to yourself and your work, this will require a whole new set of unfamiliar behaviors. Recognition requires that you be seen and heard. Think about all the people that get recognized in your organization—what do they have in common? How do they talk about themselves and their work, and how are they perceived? Gaining recognition is achievable and can be done without rocking the teamwork boat. Let's begin with the principles of recognition.

The Principles of the Seize Recognition Strategy

Two core principles define and drive recognition: *perception* and *behaviors*. First, you need to get clear on how you are currently perceived and how you want to be perceived. Then you need to identify the behaviors that will change or reinforce how you are perceived.

1. **Perception.** How are you currently perceived? When you compare that to how you want to be perceived, how much of a gap is there? How others perceive you, good or bad, is often based on unintended interpretations of our behaviors or a lack of information from which to draw a conclusion. Without specific data, examples, or your clear communication, you leave it to others to draw their own conclusions about who you are or your performance.

Diane had no clue what others thought of her. Although she felt unappreciated, she assumed that no news was good news. It was a complete surprise to her that the company wanted her to lead the disaster recovery project. How did they know she was the right person for the job? She had never really stopped to think about what others thought of her reputation. She just felt unappreciated and stuck on boring projects. She hadn't stopped to think of how she was perceived and how she wanted to be perceived until this project presented itself. As these questions bubbled up, she came to realize that she'd been completely clueless about this aspect of her work life. No wonder she wasn't receiving recognition. She didn't even know what she wanted to receive recognition for. Was it for her hard work? Her intelligence? Her reliability? Normally she would have taken on the project and seen it as being asked to do more work. However, in this role she shaped what she wanted to be recognized for.

What do *you* want to be recognized for?

2. **Behaviors.** Now that you know how you want to be perceived and can see the clear gap between the current and future state, it's time to close that gap. Plan how you want others to perceive you. This is not unlike a PR or marketing firm working on a project. The message that they want you to hear is very deliberate, from the images conveyed to the actually words used. You need to use the same approach. Get clear on the words you want associated with you, then say them and show them in your behaviors. Your words must align with your behaviors to effectively convey the message you intend.

Embarking on the disaster recovery project gave Diane an opportunity to ponder these perception questions. She determined that she wanted to be known for being thorough, fast, and reliable in her work. These were qualities that she had demonstrated before on projects, but had never really articulated explicitly as her distinguishing values. The disaster recovery project was a great opportunity for managing people's perceptions of her instead of leaving it to chance. After all, she not only wanted to be recognized for being thorough, fast, and reliable, but she also wanted to be considered for future exciting projects. For Diane, that would mean there was not only implicit but also explicit recognition for her contribution.

What behaviors will reinforce the qualities you want to be recognized for?

Why Seize Recognition?

Seize Recognition is your strategy for avoiding burnout. People who feel burned out contribute their efforts, yet they feel like things are not going anywhere for them. They feel like they are spinning their wheels, and for what? You need to clearly define what you want. Sometimes a paycheck is not enough. Maybe you want that bonus, promotion, new title, or a simple thank-you.

Additionally, seizing recognition means you are not giving away your credit to someone else who doesn't deserve it. There are plenty of bullies waiting to take your lunch money if you are not watching. Although this is not a pretty picture, it is the reality of human nature. You've probably run into enough of them in your lifetime to know that people will gladly take credit for other people's work. If you don't step up to say something, then you are vulnerable to others' making incorrect assumptions and, worse, taking credit for your accomplishments.

Is the Seize Recognition Strategy Right for You?

Recognition is one part your contribution and one part your ability to communicate your contribution. Use the following descriptions to determine whether this is the right strategy for you to create your end of work:

- *You are ready to get acknowledgment for who you are and what you've done.* If you are ready to call out your contributions and not play the odds that others just might recognize you, then Seize Recognition is your strategy. You've been ready and waiting around for that recognition from your boss and coworkers. When and if it finally comes around, you revel in it, but more would be nice. You're not too proud to admit that. You need more, and you are ready to go out there, earn it, communicate it, and have people recognize your contribution.

- *You deserve to achieve status.* If you appreciate status and titles, then Seize Recognition is the strategy for you. Many of us are too modest to admit it, but when push comes to shove, we love the recognition that comes with a certain title and salary increase. It's a reflection of our hard work and contribution, and it's acknowledgment from the organization that we've done a great job. It's something to work toward and celebrate.

- *You want something in return for your efforts.* If you want to have balance between what you contribute and what you receive, then Seize Recognition is the right strategy for you. For some of us, it's a matter of principle: organizations and managers should acknowledge their people. You feel there is something fundamentally wrong when hard work goes unnoticed and unappreciated. You go out of your way to thank others, and you expect no less in return.

If any of these three descriptions sound like you, use the Seize Recognition strategy to help you create the end of work as you know it. Seize Recognition to help you define how you want to be perceived, and go out there to get it.

Make Recognition a Reality

We've explored the definition of recognition and why you would want to use this strategy to create your end of work. Now that you've determined that the Seize Recognition strategy is the right one for you, we will explore how to bring it to life by determining how you want to be perceived and recognized, then creating an action plan to make it a reality.

DEFINE YOUR RECOGNITION

We've explored the principles behind recognition. Now it's time to craft how you want to be perceived and work toward it. Just as Diane did before her epiphany, you can leave perception and therefore recognition to chance—or you can take action to create a message that is consistent with who you are and how you want to be seen.

First, let's look at your current perception and your desired perception. On a piece of paper, write down five qualities for which you are currently known; for example, you're thorough, reliable, prompt, easygoing, and friendly. If you don't know how you're perceived, this is a great opportunity to ask some trusted colleagues.

Now, with your list of qualities, do a "flip side" exercise to assemble a complete and accurate picture of how you are currently perceived—and make sure your assumptions about this are accurate. What's the flip side of each quality? To take one example, when you are thorough, it's great, but do you also tend to be too methodical sometimes? Do you unknowingly drive people nuts when you stop meetings to go over minute details that no one else cares about? This is a time for consideration and reflection. This behavior may explain why you don't get the recognition you feel you deserve. You may be thorough, but no one acknowledges you for that because they find it annoying that you are so methodical.

Now take another look at this list of qualities and ask yourself: Is this how I want to be perceived? What is the perception I desire? Identify the five traits and skills for which you most want to be recognized. These may be the same ones you already have on your list, or you may choose to replace a few.

Congratulations! Now you know the five traits and skills for which you most want to be known and recognized.

YOUR SEIZE RECOGNITION ACTIONS

Now that you've chosen to make Seize Recognition your strategy and have defined what you want to be recognized for, let's look at the attitude and actions that will bring this strategy to life. The following application section explores ways in which you can zoom in and out to shift your attitude and take actions to make your Seize Recognition strategy a reality.

1. **Know your value.** Get clear on the value you bring to the table. Is it a focus on relentless execution or a forward-thinking perspective? Know your value at any given time. Even when someone tries to push you off kilter, stay grounded. When you know your value, people can challenge you all they want and they will never discourage you.

2. **Believe that you deserve recognition.** There's no sense in apologizing for the great things you've done. Don't let your modesty get in the way. You deserve every bit of limelight you get. When someone recognizes you, don't self-sabotage and say you didn't do that much. Be gracious and thank the person.

3. **Take what you deserve.** You can't leave what you think you deserve to chance. You are your own best advocate. Don't be shy. Seize it and enjoy it.

Where should you apply your newfound attitude? Pull out your description of how you want to be perceived. Given that there is likely a gap between that and how you are currently perceived, there's room for action.

First, identify behaviors that are consistent with the five traits and skills you identified. For instance, if you want to be perceived and recognized for being trustworthy, the behaviors you will need to manifest include staying away from gossip, doing what you say you will do, and getting back to people on time. Or if you want to be perceived and recognized for being a top sales performer in your company, then the behaviors you need to manifest include rigorously researching and understanding all your customers, calling on them at least every two weeks, and when you meet with them, asking them questions about their current concerns (instead of launching into your cool new product version). Your behaviors must align with how you want to be perceived and recognized. If they are not in alignment, you won't get what you want.

Second, create a list of the times and situations in which you will demonstrate these new behaviors, as well as your target audience. Taking the earlier example of being seen as trustworthy by not gossiping, you will demonstrate this on a regular basis to coworkers when you interact with them in the hallway. For the example of being recognized a top sales performer, you will state to your manager that you want to be the top performer this quarter and improve your chances of achieving this by doing research before a customer call and by stating to your customers how important they are to you and that you want to get them the best product and price.

Third, create a success column. That is, describe the milestones or ways in which you will know that you've succeeded at demonstrating these new behaviors. What form do you want the recognition to take? How will you know that you've gotten better at demonstrating these behaviors? For example, how do you want to be recognized by your coworkers for being trustworthy? How do you want to be recognized by your company for being a top sales performer? This is about seizing your recognition. It's important to identify the form of your recognition, so that when you see it coming, you will know your efforts have made a difference. Besides making a concerted effort to demonstrate the appropriate behaviors, there will be many times when you will need to explicitly tell your coworkers of your efforts, contributions, and achievements. You may need to tell them that you have made a conscious effort to stay focused without getting caught up in workplace drama. You'll notice that after you bring this up, they'll agree with you. Coworkers most likely will not give you this recognition without being prompted. Most people are focused on themselves. In the sales situation, you may need to do a better job of announcing your numbers before the quarter end. Seize your recognition. Get clear on how you want to be recognized, then go get it.

This strategy is more intentional than you might have initially imagined, because you are setting up a plan to make this happen versus sitting around and hoping that your boss and organization will recognize your efforts. If your desire for approval and recognition is going to create your end of work, then you can't be shy about seizing it. You need to be clear on what you want to be recognized for, do the work, and then tell them what you have accomplished.

Seizing recognition is an exciting way to create your end of work. Who doesn't want to work in an environment where there are both intrinsic and extrinsic motivations to make great contributions? When you are rewarded for your hard work, you naturally will want to maintain that level of engagement, if not do even more. You can't always rely on your boss and organization to do that for you, so you've got to do it for yourself. Stand up and seize what you deserve.

7

MAINTAIN BALANCE

CASE STUDY

Tracy has worked for the same company for almost five years. She likes her job but also realizes that her job is not everything. It is one part of her life. She is a dedicated employee, but will not work on weekends nor return emails after work. She has a family and is also working part-time on her master's degree. All these things are important to her. She is proud that she has a balanced life. Her coworkers marvel at how full her life is and how she can do it all. For Tracy, it's simple: there are many aspects to her life, and she doesn't apologize that there are a number of parts that are important to her. In turn, her manager and coworkers know what they can expect. They can depend on Tracy to deliver the results that she says she will deliver. She seems to have it all.

You don't have to choose one part of your life over another. It's all important. Maintain Balance to ensure you are meeting all your life's needs. A successful life requires that your needs inside and outside of your workplace are met. The company will continue to survive if you don't check email from home or take that phone conference while on vacation.

Is This Strategy Right for You? Maintain Balance if

- You are ready to define yourself as more than what you do for a living.

- You want to create balance between all the facets of your life.

- You need to reprioritize what is important.

When to Apply: The demands, challenges, excitement, and opportunities of work are a constant. If not kept in check, these demands can envelop every aspect of your life. Maintain Balance when you need to take a step back to identify balance, prioritize all of your life's needs, and discover what you need to do to create harmony between your work and other aspects of your life.

What Balance Will Do for You: Maintain Balance to ensure you can do everything you want to do in life. Then your job will become a place you go to that nourishes, rather than drains, your professional energy.

One of the biggest challenges in life is to get to everything you want to do. Whether it's to finish remodeling your basement, take a cooking class, rebuild an old car, write your first novel, or learn to skydive, the list is never-ending. You'll always come up with something new or different that you want to explore. The dilemma: there's simply not enough time to get to everything. Worse yet, that thing called *work* seems to always get in the way of living your life. If you are a multifaceted person with many hobbies and interests, and work is only one aspect of your life, then Maintain Balance is the right strategy for you to create your end of work. Maintaining balance helps you accommodate all the things you consider important and are committed to in your life.

What Is Balance?

Imagine your life as an exquisite art piece that makes a bold statement about life as everything you want it to be—an expression of every aspect of who you are. Every color and every stroke represents the multifaceted dimensions of your personality, interests, and all that you hold dear to you. What would this piece look like? Now is your chance to paint your masterpiece. Experience work as an integral part of your life with the explicit understanding that work is only one of the many dimensions that make up your life.

Many people feel they have to choose between making their work or personal life a priority. How did we get to this place where we feel we must choose one or the other? Those who want to experience a new paradigm of work see Maintain Balance as their strategy to recognizing and negotiating the importance of both work and their personal life—together in harmony.

Tracy, our Maintain Balance queen, is able to leave her job at a designated time that she feels is appropriate. She doesn't feel guilty for leaving at this time because she has been fully present all day. She was engaged with her projects. She gave it her best. When she leaves work at the end of the day, she steps out of one experience and into another. It's a clean-cut separation for her. She has defined the three things that are important to her (work, family, and her degree) and created appropriate time allocation for each priority, thus allowing herself to be fully engaged in each experience, as there are clear demarcations.

This particular definition of balance is based not on the assumption that there is an equal split between work and your personal life, but on making a conscious decision about what is important to you, allocating what you feel should be the appropriate amount of time and energy you devote to each area, and then, when you are in each area, being fully engaged and focused. Depending on your interests, demands, and opportunities, you will shift your balance as your world changes. Balance flows and moves in harmony with your world.

The Principles of the Maintain Balance Strategy

Two major principles form the basis of balance: *commitment* and *boundaries*. First, define what you are committed to as priorities in your life. Then define the boundaries around them—and be realistic. These principles form the basis of how to achieve the balance you desire to create your end of work.

1. **Commitments.** What are the important things in your life that you are committed to?

This may seem like a simple question, but it's not really so simple. There may be thirty things that you are important to you, but you are committed to only a handful of them. There's a difference between importance and actual commitment. Things that are important to you have lots of personal and social value, such as having fun at work, charity work, working out, spending time with friends and family, learning a new skill or content area, reading books, gardening, and so on. The things that you are committed to have deeper, personal value associated with them, because when push comes to shove and you have to make a decision about what you truly are committed to, it comes down to only a handful of things. These may be having a beautiful home, feeling a sense of accomplishment, and spending time with people you care about. When you get clear on your commitments, the chatter in your head around "I should do this or make time for that" goes away and you actually do the things you are committed to.

Tracy felt it was important to work out, earn a living, spend quality time with her family, do charity work, and finish her degree. Although all these things were important to her, she could not realistically commit to everything. She needed to earn a living. It also helped that she gained a sense of daily accomplishment from her work. She needed to spend time with her children: they needed her, and they were growing up so quickly. She needed to finish her degree. She wanted to have a sense of accomplishment and long-term earning potential. All this was a lot to have on her plate.

The working out and charity work would have to wait until the degree was finished. Once she got clear on that, she stopped beating herself up for not being in shape and not giving back to her community. By letting those items go and sticking to just her commitments, she let go of a lot of guilt. She simply knew that in two years' time, she would finish her degree and would go back to working out and charity work. In the meantime, if she got the exercise every one of us needs by playing with her children, going for daily walks with her husband and the dog, and taking the stairs instead of elevators, she would be fine with not working out at a gym.

2. **Boundaries.** What resources are you willing to allocate to your commitments?

When we think about the concept of boundaries, we think about clear lines and delineation between what's in and OK, and what's out and not OK. Why is this important? It's very easy for the commitments in your life to become out of balance—meaning there's always room for one commitment to take up more resources (time and energy) than another.

For instance, if doing a great job at work is one of your commitments, along with being a part of your children's lives, it's very easy for one to take over the other. Let's say you have a project at work that's been very demanding and interesting. It has lots of visibility from the senior leaders in the organization. So, of course, you want to do your best. You find yourself working long hours; then when you do get home, you are still thinking about the project.

The reverse is true as well. Let's say you find yourself volunteering to coach your daughter's softball team. You end up spending your work hours creating and ordering team uniforms because customer service for the uniforms is not available after work hours. Next, you are coordinating getting the new equipment. You are pondering why one of your neighbors won't let her daughter play on the team. Then you need to take off from work early to coach the team. It's very easy for the lines between your commitments to get blurred. Defining your boundaries helps you to keep them separate—and in balance.

For Tracy, it became clear that given her commitments to work, family, and school, she needed to create boundaries for each. When was work to start and end? What would happen if her employer needed her to stay later to finish a last-minute project? How would she handle that?

Everything in life is a negotiation—saying "yes" isn't the only answer. Tracy would have to acknowledge: "I understand the importance of finishing this project." Then, set her boundaries: "I need to leave to pick up my kids and then go to class." And finally, renegotiate: "Is there someone else on the team who can help? If there isn't, I can only devote one hour to it this evening after class and after the kids go to sleep. Will that be too late given the time difference for the client?" Most of us get caught up in poor work/ life boundaries because of our inability to say no (or rather, our desire to say yes) and stress ourselves. It's a choice. Most organizations will push and ask, but few of us feel like we can say no. When we do say no, it's not the end of the world. It's usually a negotiation and demonstrates a respect for boundaries.

Luckily, work, school, and family were driven by time boundaries, so life was really clear and there was little or no negotiation around certain things. Tracy's master's program was in the evenings and started at 5:00 P.M. twice a week. The children needed to be at school at a particular time, and their bedtime was 8:30 P.M. Tracy respected the time boundaries around each commitment, but more important, she created emotional boundaries—that is, she would allow herself to thoughtfully place her loved ones' critical needs above her work or school commitments. So, for instance, she wasn't going to let herself feel guilty for leaving work early to pick up her kids or attend a softball game. She wasn't going to feel guilty about not getting to her homework if one of her kids was having a meltdown. By creating clear boundaries, but also knowing when to flex those boundaries, she was able to move fluidly through life even when it threw her many curve balls. She used balance (of her commitments and boundaries) as a guide for making daily decisions that allowed her to feel fully alive in all aspects of her life.

Maintain Balance is the strategy that helps make everything that's important to you—well, important. When you choose to focus on work, work is a priority and you are in the moment. In other words, you are fully engaged in your work. When you choose to leave work and focus on your personal life, you are fully engaged in that experience and not thinking about work. You are present to the thing that matters to you right then and there: your personal endeavors. It is only after you have fully engaged with your work or your personal life that you can leave it and go to the other commitment without that nagging feeling of guilt. You are engaged, so you do your best. When you are concentrating on a work project, you give it 100 percent of your effort and focus. When you are at home with family, you are 100-percent present and engaged. This focus is the antithesis of multitasking. You are a single-tasking master. Each activity has its own time, space, and attention. Instead of feeling panicked, stressed, and fragmented, now you can feel focused.

Why Maintain Balance?

The pace and amount of activities that need to be performed in any given day can be overwhelming. The very process of taking stock of what you need to do can lead to feeling overwhelmed. The Maintain Balance strategy helps you stay focused and make wise choices about how you want to spend those twenty-four hours with maximum satisfaction.

Let's face it. There is always more you could do: learn more, work more, and accomplish more. That's a lot of pressure. Our desires and expectations are not aligned. We desire more, but know it's not realistic. This misalignment creates feelings of guilt and the ongoing "should" conversation: "I should do more." Sound familiar? Maintaining balance helps you distill what is important to you when faced with the pressures of time, people asking more from you, and your own desire to do more. Balance is there to guide you to define your priorities and allocate time and energy appropriately. It's typically the reverse: we feel like time controls us. Maintaining balance gives you back control of those twenty-four hours.

Is the Maintain Balance Strategy Right for You?

Maintaining balance is for you if you believe that you can have everything that is important to you. Why can't we have a full life that includes being both fully engaged and fulfilled by our work and fully engaged in all the activities in our personal lives that interest us? The Maintain Balance strategy is for the person who wants to experience all the wonderful and diverse things in life that make it interesting. Consider the following descriptions of someone who maintains balance as a successful end of work strategy:

- *You define yourself as more than what you do for a living.* Do you believe that work is just one outlet for expressing who you are? Some of us believe that work is a place where we come to accomplish things and demonstrate our skills. It's a place to contribute our knowledge and gain a sense of identity from that experience, but it's not the only place. Work is only one outlet; there are many others in life. Some of us get caught up in the idea that what we do for a living is the total sum of who we are. For example, when you are at a party, often people will ask what you do for a living. The conversation can even be dominated by this topic. That's because some of us spend all our time and energy devoted to our work, so work becomes our only identity in life and how we define ourselves. If you think that's untrue and believe that work is only one of several arenas in which you can contribute and define yourself, then the Maintain Balance strategy is right for you.

- *You create balance between the important facets of your life.* Do you believe that you can have it all? That somehow there's a way to achieve the right balance between work and your personal activities and interests? Although work may take up the bulk of your waking hours, you know that you could manage to do three other things that you feel are important and find interesting and engaging. If you could only figure out when you will do what and stick to it, you'd be a happy camper. Maintain Balance is the right strategy for you. It will help you clarify the things you are committed to and actually create boundaries around them to make them a reality.

- *You take a step back and reprioritize what is important.* Have you come to realize that you've been consumed by only one thing in life? Perhaps you've been so heavily focused on your career, getting ahead, and making a strong impression for the last four years in your job that you're feeling burned out. Or maybe you've been so consumed with all the drama in your life (the passing of a grandparent, the divorce of a friend, your housing situation) that you've neglected work—perhaps so much so that people have been noticing and commenting on it. Either way, it's time to take a step back and reevaluate what's important to you right now. Is your job in jeopardy? Are your friendships in jeopardy? Is your living situation in jeopardy? What's important, and what are you willing to commit to making better? Maintain Balance is the right strategy for you if you are feeling that one aspect of your life has taken so much of your time and energy that you're actually off balance and not feeling good about it.

- *You do all the things you said you've wanted to do.* Are you a dreamer? Do you yearn to do many things, because there are so many things that interest you? You feel guilty at times that work is just an afterthought; you think maybe it should be more important to you, but there are so many other things in life to do and experience. You also feel guilty that you think about or talk about all the other things you want to do, but never seem to get around to them. If this is you, then Maintain Balance is the right strategy to bring forth your interests, make commitments to them, and make them real instead of just dreaming about them.

If any of these four descriptions sound like you, use the Maintain Balance strategy to help you create the end of work as you know it. You will find your Maintain Balance strategy will help you define your commitments and create boundaries around them to make your work-life balance a reality.

Make Balance a Reality

We've explored the definition and underlying principles of maintaining balance. Now that you've determined that the Maintain Balance strategy is the right one for you to use to create the end of work as you know it, we will explore how to bring this strategy to life by first defining your commitments and boundaries and then creating an action plan to make it a reality.

DEFINE YOUR BALANCE

Use this section to define what you are actually committed to and the boundaries you will create.

First, zoom out. Take a step back and reflect on what's important to you in your life, with specific details. To use an imaginary example, first there's your work—and more specifically, your identity as a manager, the fix-it gal, or the high achiever in the group. Then there's your music—more specifically, your weekend gigs. There's your body—specifically, your desire to stay in shape.

And your love of the outdoors—specifically, your long weekend bike rides.

Get the idea? Which do you hold important to you? Make a list, in detail.

Now the second part: although these things may be important to you, are you *committed* to all of them? Your music may be a lot of fun, but is it something you are committed to? You *can* do everything that's important to you if you decide to commit to every item. But be realistic. How much time and energy do you actually have? Are you truly attached and drawn to all these items on your list? Circle the ones you are truly committed to.

Remember our story of Tracy? It was important to her to do charity work, work out at the gym, spend time with her family, do a good job at work, and finish her degree. Well, when she had to get clear on her most important commitments, they really boiled down to work, family, and her degree. She clarified her commitments, got over the guilt, and moved on to being fully engaged in what she was committed to.

Now that you've gotten clear on your commitments, let's create boundaries around them. What kind of boundaries? Resource boundaries, such as time and energy spent in a particular area. We separate time and energy because there may be certain things in your life that require time, but not mental or emotional energy. For instance, if you are committed to working out four times a week for an hour and a half, that's a big chunk of your personal time, but it's not emotionally or mentally draining. Here's another example: if you have always wanted to write a novel, it requires not only time but also lots of mental and emotional energy. Let's say you've determined that you need to devote at least two hours every morning to writing (before you go to work). You are thinking and researching tons of information. That's a lot of mental energy. Finally, you beat yourself up for having writer's block on occasion. That's emotional energy.

As you take a look at the list of commitments that you've circled, think about the time that is required for you to be fully engaged with the activities associated with each commitment. Remember, full engagement also requires mental and emotional energy. For each commitment you've circled, create what you think are appropriate times you can allocate to that commitment and indicate when it's OK to focus on your commitment and when it's not OK. These boundaries will help you in contingency planning, because situations will arise that will test your boundaries. For Tracy, this may involve having to choose between the last-minute project thrown on her desk and studying for finals. Tracy's commitment is to her schoolwork in the evenings, so if work impedes on something as important as finals, then the answer is absolutely no. If it impedes on normal study time, she still says no unless it is absolutely dire. That is, there is no one else who can take on the project, it cannot wait until the morning, or it will jeopardize her job. Most of the time, we like to be heroes and imagine that we are the only ones who can do the job, it cannot wait until the morning, or that we will get fired for saying no. This is not always the truth. When you are clear on your boundaries, the choice of what to do and what to focus on will be clear. This will enable you to stick to your desired balance.

YOUR MAINTAIN BALANCE ACTIONS

Now that you've chosen to make Maintain Balance your strategy for how to end work as you know it, it's time to make it a reality. Let's look at the attitude and actions that will bring it to life. This application section explores ways in which you can zoom in and out to shift your attitude and take actions to make balance a reality in your life.

Here are three helpful attitude tips:

1. **Remain both steadfast and flexible.** Your balance will constantly be put to the test as the demands of everyday life come up. You will encounter unexpected changes. When this happens, stay steadfast on your commitments and boundaries—and also realize that there may have to be

exceptions. Leave yourself some room to be flexible if need be. Although it seems contradictory to be both steadfast and flexible, these are important attitudes to keep in mind. Others will experience you as more effective when you can do both.

2. **Be good to yourself (and don't beat yourself up).** Life is a series of negotiations. In your effort to remain steadfast and flexible, keep in mind that something will have to give. This is not necessarily a bad thing. People who experience optimized balance don't beat themselves up over small things. They get to do everything they truly want to because they are willing to let go of something else and still feel fulfilled. So be good to yourself.

3. **Be steady.** You can choose to go through your day frenzied, trying to get to everything, or go through your day calm, but still trying to get to everything. At the end of the day, you'll have gotten to whatever you got to—how you go about doing it dictates your experience. When you are steady and calm, your experience will be more pleasant, as will the experience of those around you.

Where should you apply your newfound attitude? Pull out your list of priorities again. Look at your commitments and the boundaries you've created. How do the three attitudes just presented affect the way you will go about expressing your balance?

First, to whom do you need to communicate your balance? Do these include specific members of your family, your boss, and your closest friends?

Second, what underlying attitude will you bring to the conversation that will affect how you will have each of these conversations? With your partner or spouse, will you need to remain steadfast and flexible? With your boss, will you need to be prepared to not be defensive or beat yourself up and feel guilty if she tells you she is disappointed that you are not willing to sacrifice everything? With your friends, do you need to make sure you hold your ground and negotiate other options for how to spend time together?

Third, what requests do you need to make of the people in your life to help you stick to your commitments and boundaries? As you prepare to share with others your Maintain Balance strategy for creating your end of work, what do you need these important people in your life to do for you to help keep you on track? You may find that you have to ask your partner or spouse to not lay the guilt trip on you and, more important, to accept the decisions you make. You may have to ask your boss to realize that when you say no to something it's not because you don't care.

To bring your desired balance into your life may upset the current balance, but this is an important milestone in your life that requires you to be strong and stand up for what you truly want. The people around you may be initially uncomfortable with the change, but the long-term advantage far outweighs the short-term discomfort.

Live the Maintain Balance strategy to get clear on what you're committed to, and create boundaries to make balance an everyday part of your life. This is your chance to create a lasting way of experiencing all the things in life that are important to you. As humans, we interpret our experiences to give them meaning and significance. When you work through your Maintain Balance strategy and experience the difference in your life, you will find that everything you do lives up to its full potential.

8

BUILD
LEGACY

John knows the analytical and technical skills that he brings to each company. For the last eight years, he has worked in three companies, and in each situation he's been known as the "fix-it" guy for business process improvement. He makes companies more efficient, faster, and fiscally sound. Not surprisingly, word of his success would get out, headhunters would track him down, the calls would start, and he'd be courted by a new company. With each company for whom he's worked, John knows the results that he is going to leave behind and what he will take from the experience. By the time John is through with a company, he has identified and implemented new business processes. John's results create such impact that once they are up and running, he knows that they will not only save the company time and money, but also stay intact long after he has left. For John, legacy is the goal, not longevity of employment. The more companies he can positively affect, the better.

Build your legacy to balance what you give and take from your job. When you are clear on your desired legacy, you zero in on what you want to create today, next week, and next year, and the mark you will leave behind. In return, what you take from creating your legacy is a sense of professional accomplishment, new skills, and résumé-building experiences.

Is This Strategy Right for You? Build Legacy if

- You strive for balance between what you contribute and take from your job.

- You want to leave your mark no matter the environment, challenges, or outcome.

- You want to ensure you get a return for your efforts.

- You need to define the links that connect multiple jobs and careers into a coherent path.

When to Apply: Build Legacy to get clear on "What's in it for me?" This strategy is great for emergency morale-boosting during those existential "Why am I working here?" crisis moments, as well as longer-term career trajectory defining endeavors. The Build Legacy strategy is potent when used to define tangible results in the face of vague situations, and it is a powerful medicine to bring to light and connect your contribution across multiple projects, jobs, and careers.

What Building Legacy Will Do for You: Build Legacy to identify the common thread that links together hundreds of projects, multiple jobs, and years of experience. When you know what your legacy is, you will automatically steer toward the right opportunities, understand the significance of your work, and shape your perspective to see the value you contribute on a daily basis for the rest of your life.

Imagine living life as an ongoing game of musical chairs. Every time you come to a new project or job, you never know if you'll be left at the end without a chair and, more important, with nothing to show for all those years of service. Wouldn't that be awful? If you've been experiencing work as a no-win game, it's no wonder you feel disconnected or even bitter about work. You've been working for someone else. It's time to build your legacy into everything you do so that every project, job, and career fits into the bigger scheme of who you are and the mark you want to make.

What Is Legacy?

One of the biggest challenges in the midst of everyday work life is defining how your efforts reflect *you* both in the moment and over your lifetime. Every workplace offers us the opportunity to develop new skills, learn about ourselves, and have experiences that become the stories of our successes or the challenges we overcame. Sadly, we rarely step back to put these experiences and opportunities into perspective. Days, weeks, years, projects, and jobs simply glom together like some protoplasmic blob. Without understanding what you contribute or gain from your effort, everything coalesces into a collective blur. We have come to accept this lack of distinction as normal. However, what we have come to consider *normal* is not always the best thing for us.

Build your legacy as a strategy when you want to both take and give more to your job. The Build Legacy strategy helps clarify and put into action what is important to you. When you establish your legacy, you see the intentional impact and contribution that you create in each of your jobs and the experience and learning you take with you. This is not just a singular process in which you pretend that you are deceased and are looking back on your life. Shelve the embalming fluid. This strategy puts you on a forward-facing trajectory.

When you know what you want your legacy to be, you have focus, direction, and motivation in everything you do at work. Your work will have a fundamentally deeper meaning because you know how your work relates to what you want to create. Your legacy reflects what is unique about who you are, what you know, what you want to be known for, and how you want to be remembered.

The legacy you create as part of your professional path reflects your unique skills and abilities. For process guru John, it was creating systems to automate manufacturing and procurement processes. He knew these systems would make a tremendous impact and be around long after he'd left the company. Not only did he provide the company with a streamlined process, but he also took things from the experience that made his résumé stronger (as evidenced by the constant flood of calls from recruiters). Your legacy contribution can take many forms, including introducing new ways to get work done, a new product or service idea, or even influencing how coworkers collaborate. What you want in return for your contribution is also entirely up for grabs.

The Principles of the Build Legacy Strategy

Two major principles form the basis of the Build Legacy strategy. Whether you are relatively new to the workforce or a veteran of many decades, it is important to understand these two elements. They are *knowing what you take from your job* and *knowing what you give to it*. They are both equally important; therefore they must be balanced.

When you take more from your job and work experience than you give, you may have this nagging guilty feeling. Questions like "I guess I could do more, but why?" will often come up. That's not a fulfilling way in which to experience work. Who among us would want to go to work knowing we are not maximizing our potential or feeling like we are not being honest with ourselves or our employer? On the other hand, when we give more than we take, we feel like we are being taken advantage of, and we finally realize that we could quickly burn out. Too much of one thing is simply not good.

Here's a deeper dive into the two principles.

1. **Taking.** What do you want from your current job and what do you want to take with you when you leave?

You may be thinking to yourself, "Taking? Isn't work about what I'm *producing* for my employer?" Sure, if you want to experience work as something that will burn you out or, even worse, as a prison in which you are stuck. Work has tension when we feel that we are working toward the goals of someone else, and not our own. The Build Legacy strategy—specifically, the "take" principle—is what will allow you to break this vicious cycle. We are not suggesting that you go and figure out a way to work for yourself, although that may be something you will or can pursue. Instead, we are suggesting that you can also try to create your end of work in your current employment situation. So look at your current situation and determine how you can also get more from the experience.

John wasn't happy initially with his reputation as the fix-it guy. He thought it just meant he would be stuck with projects that were problematic. He realized that he needed to make sure he got something for himself out of the experience. Besides a steady paycheck, John needs to be stimulated. He gets bored easily, so it's important to him that his work be stimulating. He also sees his work as a place for him to improve his skills and learn new things. Finally, when pushed he will admit that he's very proud to have his executive title. That made all the problem projects worth it. These are all the things John takes from his job.

Are there ways for you to take more from your work? Yes! Here are some ways in which you can get more from your projects and job. Your projects, your job, or both can help you build stronger skills or even a new set of skills. Take advantage of that and find ways in which to build your skills, whether through formal training or learning from others who have more experience or a different set of experiences. Your current project or job can help you network with people. We all know that stronger relationships and a larger network of colleagues will serve you in both the short and long-term. Your current project or job can help you build your résumé and make you more marketable long-term. If your current projects aren't helping you grow, take the initiative to look for other appropriate projects and speak up on your behalf to your manager. There are many ways in which you can take more from your current project and job. Get clear on what these are for you.

   2. Giving. What will you *contribute* to your employer? What will you give and what will live on after you have left?

Legacy is also about what you contribute to your employer in a meaningful way. It's not enough to go to work, do your job, and clock out. If you want to end work as you know it, you have to contribute in a way that makes you feel good and proud.

John feels it is important to contribute to his company in a meaningful way and to leave a lasting impact. This is his own personal value. His parents taught him to work hard, and he's applied those working values to his job and career. He's proud to tell his kids that along with his title come responsibilities that he lives up to. Companies hire him to solve problems related to their internal financial operations, and that's what he does. He has a knack for finding the breakdowns and inefficiencies, and he's not afraid to make the most of his skills.

Think about what makes you unique. Is it your organizational skills? Is it your big-picture skills? Or maybe it's your in-depth knowledge of a field. This is your chance to bring your unique skills to the table and contribute in a way that will affect the company short- or long-term.

If you build your legacy to create your end of work, you accept that you balance both what you take from your work and what you give to it. Your definition of legacy may also continually evolve as you and your life evolve. Some components of your life will change, including your jobs, interests, projects, coworkers, careers, professional objectives, what's important to you, and maybe even your legacy. But your values will remain a constant. Use your values to guide you as your legacy shifts from one stage of your life to another. Legacy is a means to bring forth who you are and what's important to you, no matter the circumstances.

Build your legacy as a strategy to define exactly what you want to contribute to each experience and what you want in return.

Why Build Legacy?

Your Build Legacy strategy helps you stay focused and distill what is important to you when faced with multiple options such as projects, work relationships, training opportunities, companies to work for, and overall career choices. This strategy is there to guide you to define and leave *your* mark so you have something to show for all your hard work. Building your legacy increases your sense of accomplishment and control.

Furthermore, building your legacy creates a powerful framework that defines what you will create and achieve each day, each project, each job, and throughout your lifetime. Legacy connects the threads between our values, desires, experiences, jobs, and projects. For John, his contribution reflects expertise coupled with a desire to keep building his résumé.

Build your legacy to define what's unique about what you bring to everything you do. Your definition of what makes you unique allows you to clearly see how your contributions can make a powerful short-term or long-lasting impact on the company. In the stormy environment of today's cube farms, it's more and more of a challenge to see the results and impact of our work. Remember that last project you poured your heart into that went nowhere? What about the second reorganization for the year? The teammates who constantly challenge your sanity? Despite all these workplace distractions, you can use your legacy to help you see the big picture and, equally important, as a structure to guide your actions. The structure will keep you focused so you can make a positive impact and see the results of your contribution despite the chaos.

Build your legacy to also help you define what you need in return in the short- and long-term. In the midst of the blur of time spent at work, the Build Legacy strategy is the map that guides you to find substance in the call center reorg project or the massive fifty-page presentation that you know will require prolonged consensus to complete. The goal of your legacy is to provide a beacon that helps you find a stable base of sanity by reinforcing what you are going to give to this project and what's in it for you. Perhaps you take with you the fact that you built stronger relationships with coworkers, remained patient in the depth of consensus despair, and finally figured out how to most effectively budget your time on complex projects. With your legacy as your guide, you make sure you get something out of every project that will make your résumé or skill sets stronger. Even if the team is mired in ambiguity, you are clear on what you are contributing and what you can take from this experience.

Is the Build Legacy Strategy Right for You?

The Build Legacy strategy is for you if you care about making a visible impact in the world and the contributions you make in the context of your work. Consider the following aspects that are important to those who make Build Legacy their end of work strategy:

- *You strive for balance between what you contribute to and take from your job.* Do you care about a fair exchange between you and your employer? For some people, it's important that it's an even deal. When the balance is off, some of us become resentful of the hard work we put forth and the lack of return. When you strive for balancing what you give and take in the Build Legacy strategy, you are considering how your previous, current, and even future work contributes to the bigger picture of who you are as a person and the mark you want to leave behind. So if it's important to you that in your workplace you get back as much as you give—whether it's in the form of personal satisfaction, pride, recognition, or compensation—the Build Legacy strategy is right for you. It will help you get clear on what you need in return for all that you give, so that you reach your end of work.

- *You want to leave your mark no matter the environment, challenges, or outcome.* If you care about your long-term impact on the company, industry, or people around you, then it's likely you care about your legacy. Your lasting impact on others is something you take pride in. If this notion of lasting impact is important to you, then the Build Legacy strategy is right for you.

- *You need to define the links that connect multiple jobs and careers into a coherent path.* If you have had an amazing career that has led you through a series of widely varying work pursuits, and you have found all the experiences satisfying, then the Build Legacy strategy will help you tie it all together so you effectively build on your experiences. In short, none of it was wasted effort; ultimately, all of it adds to the whole of your legacy. Although your careers and jobs may seem disparate, you are clear there's something important and enduring that drives you down each path. Your Build Legacy strategy will help you find the common thread in what you've been doing.

If any of these three descriptions sound like you, use the Build Legacy strategy to help you create the end of work as you know it. You will find that your Build Legacy strategy helps you redefine work on your terms because you are clear on the level of impact you want to leave in your industry, profession, or organization. You'll take control to make work fit into how you want to remember work and be remembered for your work.

Make Legacy a Reality

We've explored the definition and underlying principles of legacy. Now that you've determined that building your legacy is the right strategy for you to use to create the end of work as you know it, we will explore how to bring your Build Legacy strategy to life by first defining your own desired legacy and then creating an action plan to make it a reality.

DEFINE YOUR LEGACY

With each experience, we leave behind the impression of who we are, regardless of our intent. Think about the last time you were handed yet another project at the last minute with no rationale. Suddenly this was your priority. And just for a little icing on the cake, it was due . . . yesterday. You scrambled like a mad person to get the work completed. Your boss was either impressed that you rose to the occasion and delivered a great report—or nonchalant. Whether your boss's reaction was ecstatic or not worth remembering, what is important is that you stepped up and did what was in line with your legacy. When you are clear on your legacy, everything matters, because everything contributes to achieving your legacy.

Use the following questions to help you think through what's important to you and where you've been. Here you'll use your zooming-out skills. As you go through this exercise, consider your daily activities and interactions, as well as the bigger picture of your job and career. Looking at your collective experience, consider the following three questions:

1. **Values.** What are the top three values that I want to bring to my work?

Examples of values include honesty, integrity, determination, reliability, consistency, and compassion. Your short- and long-term career trajectories are focused when you know how your actions fit within the values you have identified. Ambiguity vanishes when you are clear on the values you bring to work. You have clarity on what decisions to make, how to work with others, and your overall standards.

2. **Reputation.** How do people currently perceive me and how do I want to be perceived?

It's easy to say to yourself that you don't care—or need to care—what other people think. After all, isn't this about creating your own end of work, not someone else's? True, this is about you; however, you want to be sure to leave the mark you want, not an unintended one. Understand how others perceive you and how you want to be perceived, and identify actions to align these perceptions. Note: This is about alignment, not proving that you are a nonconformist. A positive reputation makes it easier to create your legacy. For example, are you currently considered difficult to work with because you are nitpicky about details? Go back to your values. Are you being nitpicky because it's important to you that people can rely on the quality of your work? If so, then reliability needs to be a part of your reputation. But you can make a few behavioral changes to transform this perception from negative to positive. For example, you can lay off going into the details in front of other people and just make the corrections yourself without making a big deal out of it, or perhaps you can take the time to explain to others what's important to you rather than blasting them for being careless.

3. **Common theme.** What is the common theme that weaves together all of my experiences?

One of the most important aspects to consider when you build legacy is that it heightens awareness of what you contribute to every interaction. Where once there was ambiguity, now there is intent and clarity on how your actions fit into a larger context. You will be able to look back and see the commonalities of what you have contributed and gained across multiple interactions, projects, and jobs.

Now that you've zoomed out and considered these three background questions, you can zoom in and look at actually crafting your legacy statement. To do this, we go back to the principles of give and take.

- What do I want to contribute?

- What do I want to take with me?

Given your values, your current and desired reputation, and the theme(s) in your career, who are you and what do you stand for? For example, you are a hard-working individual who cares about providing quality work (this is your value). As a result, it's not surprising that you are known for being the fix-it person (this is your reputation). In fact, you've made a career out of fixing broken things (this is your career link). It would be natural to assume that your legacy is about fixing things. Well, that's a good start, but it's not compelling enough.

You want to feel good about your legacy, not about showing up to work to fix problems that others have created. Put a positive spin on something that could be seen as negative or cause you concern. Perhaps your legacy is about "making things whole." How you contribute to your employer is to make things whole and right again by providing comprehensive, quality solutions. What you get from this is the experience of knowing you've made something stronger and that it will continue to serve the company long after you're gone. "Making things whole" is a compelling legacy. John's legacy statement could be, "My contribution to the workplace and every organization I work with is to make it whole in such a way that the people and systems are aligned and functioning optimally."

Play around with the ideas and wording for your legacy. This exercise might take you a few moments or it could take you a lifetime. If you want to make Build Legacy your strategy to end work as you know it, we suggest you compose your legacy statement soon. Talk your ideas over with a trusted person in your life who can provide you with feedback, insights, and suggestions. Also keep in mind that your legacy can change as you achieve your goals, change jobs, and grow as a person. Remember to balance what you give and take. If you give too much and take too little in return, you will feel underappreciated, burned out, frustrated, and a prisoner of your own cubicle. In contrast, if you take too much without giving back, others might see you as thinking you're entitled to more than your rightful share. Once you've gotten clear on your legacy, move on to the next section to build legacy in your projects, jobs, and career.

YOUR BUILD LEGACY ACTIONS AND YOUR PROJECTS

Picture a task that you abhor. That one thing that somehow—despite your dodging, crafty avoidance, and attempts to hand off to unwary coworkers—you still must face. You know what tasks we are talking about—the ones you deem tedious and beneath you: that report, the presentation review, the documentation of Stanley's inappropriate poor behavior, or your supervisor's insistence on thorough documentation of your weekly tasks, results, and eating habits—the lowly tasks that you thought your college degree would abolish from your life, yet you are still cursed to perform. Pick one of these.

Now think about your legacy: how would you change your behavior when it comes to tasks and projects? Perhaps you might see this task as a rite of passage, a challenge, or simply a necessary part of the job. Even the most seemingly interesting job has tasks that are tedious. The neurosurgeon must fill out lengthy surgery logs; the Alaskan crab fisherman must clean the decks. Everyone needs to do things that rank as boring along with the fun parts that create career joy.

With your Build Legacy strategy, you see that, for example, writing a report gives you an opportunity to gain visibility with senior executives, so you make sure that report reflects your capabilities. Remember, when you see the world through your legacy lens, you see the opportunities, not challenges, in the things you are asked to do. You zoom out to see that you are doing it in service of something bigger. Your motivation to write the report increases because you see it as an opportunity to shine and, more important, you zoom in to get it done (without resentment) and get it done well!

YOUR BUILD LEGACY ACTIONS AND YOUR JOB

You wake up every morning and drag yourself out of bed. You know those mornings when every second of sleep is more precious than the last and you can't hit the snooze button enough times. Have you considered why it's so hard to get out of bed? Most of us (remember the Gallup stat of 71 percent) are not engaged with our jobs. Work is there to pay the bills. However, as part of your end of work adventure, you're learning that there is more to work than simply paying the bills. Your job is an extension of you and your interests; it's a conduit for your larger objectives. Now think about your legacy. If you live by your three legacy actions, what behaviors can you change to create your legacy?

Perhaps you start to see the job as something more than just a way to generate paychecks. It's the place to create and live your legacy. Your job becomes an amazing opportunity to get what you need from it. Your job is more than just a job; it's actually an integrated part of your life and who you are. Your job provides you with opportunities to learn, grow, and expand your marketability as a professional. If your legacy is to leave the world with your foolproof accounting system, your job becomes your lab. As you build and create your system, you will be recognized in the company and industry as a pioneer.

YOUR BUILD LEGACY ACTIONS AND YOUR CAREER

Let's zoom out and take a look at legacy and your big picture. Your legacy future requires you to reflect on what brought you to today. Reflect on your current career trajectory from the thirty-thousand-foot perspective.

If you have been in the workforce for a while, consider your last three jobs. If you have always been at the same company or are new to the workforce, think about three projects or three unique environments that you have been a part of, such as college, your car club, and your band. What did you bring to each of those experiences? What skills did you offer, and what contributions did you make? Look at the similarities across all three. Consider knowledge or information, personality or attitude, or maybe work ethic. The similarities will help you begin to see the common themes in what you consistently contribute. Do you see patterns of pushing the envelope? Do you see patterns of being conservative and consistent? Perhaps you notice that you have a tendency to make the environment around you more fun. The benefit of looking back is the chance to define your accomplishments, strengths, and successes, and the elements that connect your contribution across projects, jobs, and careers. This information will arm you for taking a look at the part of your career that lies ahead.

It may be hard to imagine where you will be years from now. There are so many possibilities, opportunities, and serendipitous events that will lead you down many paths. The time will pass quickly, and before you know it you will be looking back on what you have accomplished. Let's look toward your future. What do you want to leave behind and take with you in your career, given where you've been?

This is your opportunity to tap into what drives and motivates you. Now your job is a vehicle to accomplish your objectives. This is your legacy! Build Legacy to focus on what you want to contribute and gain every day from work. Your legacy is the mark you leave in the world and what you gain in return for your contribution. As you see, hear, and experience the world through your Build Legacy strategy, you will cut through the noise and distractions to target exactly what you want to contribute and gain in every situation. This is your route to creating the end of work as you know it.

Remember, on the road to your end of work you will encounter challenges, excitement, and self-discovery. That's great! Just remember that your legacy is your guide, and it's up to you to make the most out of every situation. After all, the end goal is not happiness, but to feel alive in what you do professionally. You now work toward your own goals as well the goals of your employer. It's equitable. It's your living legacy.

CONCLUSION

Now that the journey of reading this book is coming to a close, the real work begins. It's such a cliché, but it's hard not to acknowledge this fact. Why does the work start now? Along with choosing one or more strategies that resonate with you comes the work of applying that strategy as you live your life and see your daily experiences through a new lens. Whether you choose one strategy or more, you are making the commitment to shift your attitude and behaviors toward work. Take a moment to think carefully about what those new attitudes and behaviors will look like. Write them down. Find ways to implement those new behaviors in your world. It's up to you to keep it going.

If you find, with time, that the strategy you've chosen isn't hitting home anymore, consider the following: perhaps it's not that the strategy is no longer effective, but that it is no longer relevant to you. You've changed, or your circumstances have changed, or both. If so, you may have to shift your strategy.

If you are at a relatively early point in your career, you may find that certain things like learning new skills and advancing your career are more important to you. If you are midcareer, you may find that being recognized by your organization for your hard work is a rarity and therefore what you need right now. And if you are in the later stages of your career, you may find that you are thinking about the lasting impact and contributions you have made to your organization and industry. The strategy choices are different for different people at different times in their lives.

Last Words

We'd like to offer some final words about implementation of your new strategy—particularly, three things to be aware of and some pitfalls to avoid.

First, as you go out into the world and actively engage with work in a new way, people will wonder what's gotten into you. Did someone say something to you, or did you just become a more engaged person on your own? This is a compliment. The fact that people are noticing a shift in your attitude and behavior means that you are doing something right. It's not a shameful thing to admit to others that you've done some reflecting and have become clear about what's important to you in the workplace. You don't have to disclose stories of epiphanies and resolutions. Remember, it's a compliment, so thank those who notice your new attitude, and keep doing what you're doing.

Second, just because you've suddenly become the hotshot in your office and gotten the attention of senior leaders doesn't mean you have a license to judge others for toiling like drones in their cubicles. This is the second pitfall to avoid. Your coworkers are not as fortunate to have picked up this book or even thought about helping themselves out of their current situation. Be kind and compassionate, and hope that they find their path.

Third, pay it forward. No, we don't mean the book (but we certainly wouldn't discourage your getting the word out). What we mean is, share your experience, insights, and learning with others. When the time is right and you are in a place of generosity (not arrogance), be a mentor or guide to others who are struggling with work. You will undoubtedly encounter many people in your lifetime who are struggling in their careers, struggling with the idea of working, and even questioning working for someone else. You may hear them talking about quitting their job to start a bakery or a consultancy or a nonprofit. All these ventures are admirable and have potential to serve as the person's end of work. These ventures also require an incredible amount of work, perseverance, and entrepreneurial spirit. Some people find that exhilarating. Others find it scary. Regardless of the path they take, the most important questions that you can ask are the following: "What will the end of work look like for you? Could you find it or create it in your current scenario? Or will it take a complete shift for you to create your end of work?" This is where you can truly pay it forward and help make a difference to someone else.

The Final Conclusion—Really

In summary, creating your end of work is up to you. No one is going to hand you the perfect job. You are not going to wake up and discover that life has magically changed by itself. It is in your hands to make a difference in your life.

But we leave you in good hands. There's no one out there better suited than *you* to look after your career, professional satisfaction, and overall happiness. Only you truly have the best intentions for yourself. We are honored to have been here to help guide you in the right direction. May your end of work adventures take you to places you have only dreamed of . . . or never even dreamed of before.

RESOURCES

This section is designed to provide you with further resources that can help you along your end of work path.

Print Resources

Bolles, Richard Nelson. *What Color Is Your Parachute?: A Practical Manual for Job-Hunters and Career-Changers.* Berkeley, California: Ten Speed Press, updated annually.

This is a classic. For the times when you are in between jobs and trying to create your next end of work, this is an obvious choice to help you think through different options for long-term success.

———. *What Color Is Your Parachute? Workbook.* Berkeley, California: Ten Speed Press, 2005.

The workbook is a useful complement to the main *Parachute* book. It's always nice to be able to answer thought-provoking questions by writing them down on paper.

Brandon, Rick, and Marty Seldman. *Survival of the Savvy: High-Integrity Political Tactics for Career and Company Success.* New York: Free Press, 2004.

We have talked a lot about understanding the nuances in your organization and the politics as part of bringing your end of work strategy to life. This is a strong resource as it helps you think about the dimensions of politics. It's particularly helpful for those who feel that office politics can feel so negative, even dirty at times. It reframes how being savvy is important to success.

Goldsmith, Marshall. *What Got You Here Won't Get You There.* New York: Hyperion, 2007.
This best-selling book is full of important information about understanding your own patterns and what gets in the way of your future and long-term success. Even if you aren't a leader who's climbing the corporate ladder, this book has helpful lessons for everyone.

Riso, Don Richard, and Russ Hudson. *The Wisdom of the Enneagram: The Complete Guide to Psychological and Spiritual Growth for the Nine Personality Types.* New York: Bantam, 1999.
Where did our end of work strategies come from? The Enneagram is an ancient personality system on which some aspects of the end of work are based. We found that although there are nine personality styles, there are overlaps in what each personalities would consider the end of work. Use this book to identify the core drivers of your personality—but you have to be prepared to be really honest with yourself when reading through this. This system was designed for you to be the ultimate judge of which personality type best reflects you, but our experience has found sometimes people around you can more easily and accurately type you than you can. Sometimes we just have blinders on, so it can be helpful to get other's input to most accurately type yourself. Once you've determined your type, it will open up lots of room for growth and understanding which end of work choice will serve you best.

Scott, Cynthia. *Managing Change at Work, Third Edition: Leading People Through Organizational Transitions.* Ontario, Canada: Crisp Learning, 2004.

All of the end of work strategies ask for some level of change in both yourself and how you impact your environment, but there are many other things to be aware of in the change process—from the emotional component for yourself and others (denial, resistance, exploration, and commitment) to the structural aspects of change (analysis, design, implementation, and execution). This resource will help you each step of the way.

Sindell, Milo, and Thuy Sindell. *Job Spa: 12 Weeks to Refresh, Refocus, and Recommit to Your Career.* Avon, Massachusetts: Adams Media, 2008.

This prescriptive book helps you become more engaged with your job. After you've decided to create your end of work, you may need extra help on a week-by-week basis to implement your new end of work ideas and principles.

———. *Sink or Swim: New Job. New Boss. 12 Weeks to Get It Right.* Avon, Massachusetts: Adams Media, 2006.

If you have tried everything you can to create your end of work with your current employer and have found that there are fundamental differences you cannot live with, then it may be time to move on. When you do move on, *Sink or Swim* is a great resource to support you in the first twelve weeks of your new job. It helps you to decode the organizational culture and prepares you week-by-week for long-term success, which includes implementing your end of work strategies from the very beginning.

Internet Resources

Hit the Ground Running
www.HitTheGroundRunning.com

This is a website that provides three products to help business professionals at various stages of their careers—from starting a job (Sink or Swim), to being more engaged on the job (Job Spa), to leaving a job (The Last 90 Days). More specifically:

Sink or Swim (online version)

If you have tried everything you can to create your end of work with your current employer and have found that there are fundamental differences you cannot live with, then it may be time to move on. When you do move on, Sink or Swim is a great resource to help you in the first twelve weeks of your new job. It helps you to decode the organizational culture and prepare you week-by-week for long-term success, which includes implementing your end of work strategies from the very start. Sometimes you just need help translating the ideas of a book into action. Sink or Swim, the online version, helps you determine week-by-week the tasks you need to perform to be successful from the start. It also contains various dynamic tools including a goal tracking tool to help you stay focused.

Job Spa (online version)

This is a great companion guide to the book, helping you become more engaged with your current job. After you've decided to create your end of work, you may need extra help on a week-by-week basis to implement your new end of work ideas and principles. This is exactly what Job Spa does. This online version helps you determine week-by-week the tasks you need to perform to reach your goals. It also contains various dynamic tools including a Personal PR Plan tool to help you manage how others perceive you and a goal tracking tool to help you stay focused.

The Last 90 Days (online version)

If you do decide that greener employment pastures lie beyond the walls of your current employer and Build Legacy is your end of work strategy, then this is a great tool to transition out while reinforcing your legacy. This program provides a step-by-step plan for leaving your mark effectively.

Knowledge Genie
www.MyKnowledgeGenie.com

Knowledge Genie is a software platform that allows subject-matter experts to capture, package, and publish what they know. If you are working on a project and need to educate your customers or employees as part of your end of work strategy, this is an easy tool for you to get information out to others quickly—whether it's your new idea for a change in the company or wanting to leave a legacy and transfer your knowledge. Or, if you are thinking that you may want to try the entrepreneurial route, this is a great way to get your knowledge out in the world and monetize what you know.

Marshall Goldsmith Professional Success System
www.MyMGPro.com

If you are a leader and think you need extra help to become more engaged with your work, this is a great interactive tool based on Goldsmith's book *What Got You Here Won't Get You There*. This website helps you identify areas for improvement and build credibility with other professional contacts.

UpMo
www.upmo.com

This career service website is designed to help you manage your career. There are tons of great resources available on this site to help you create a plan for success and track your progress.

INDEX

ABOUT THE AUTHORS

Milo Sindell

Milo Sindell is the cofounder of two software companies: Knowledge Genie, a software company that transforms how people and organizations capture, package, and publish what they know; and Hit The Ground Running, specializing in employee performance.

Milo is also an expert and entrepreneur in the field of organization and employee performance. He has worked for leading organizations including Intel and Sun Microsystems. He has published several books and numerous articles in the field of employee performance and talent management. These books include *Sink or Swim: New Job. New Boss. 12 Weeks to Get It Right* and *Job Spa: 12 Weeks to Refresh, Refocus, and Recommit to Your Career.*

As the cofounder of Hit The Ground Running, he developed software to increase employee performance and retention in three critical stages of the employee lifecycle: starting a job, being engaged on the job, and leaving the job. Milo then leveraged his software platform to launch a first-of-its-kind program that transforms the one-to-one coaching methodology of one of the world's foremost experts on leadership, Marshall Goldsmith, into a virtual coaching program (www.myMGpro.com). He then cofounded Knowledge Genie to enable others to create similar web applications for themselves.

Thuy Sindell, PhD

Thuy Sindell is the cofounder of two software companies: Knowledge Genie, a publishing platform that helps experts capture, package, and publish what they know into a Web app; and Hit The Ground Running, specializing in employee performance. She also specializes in leadership and employee development. She has spent her career focused on helping employees take ownership of their career and demonstrate successes by learning to decode the culture and expectations of their unique organizations. This experience has culminated in her coauthoring two previous career books: *Sink or Swim: New Job. New Boss. 12 Weeks to Get it Right*, and *Job Spa: 12 Weeks to Refresh, Refocus, and Recommit to Your Career.*

In her work as a leadership consultant and coach with Mariposa Leadership, Inc., Thuy has worked with managers and their teams to develop their leadership skills in the areas of strategic thinking, influencing, and coaching skills. She is known for helping her clients gain clarity on what is expected of them as leaders and build skills to effectively fulfill their roles. Thuy's work has resulted in marked behavioral changes as well as bottom-line impact. Her clients have included Fortune 500 and industry-leading companies such as Apple, Charles Schwab, Cisco Systems, Gap, Hewlett-Packard, Ricoh Silicon Valley, Scios (a Johnson & Johnson company), Silicon Graphics Inc., Sun Microsystems, VeriSign, University of California, Berkeley, Wells Fargo, and Yahoo!

Visit www.MyKnowledgeGenie.com.

Notes

Notes

MORE BUSINESS AND CAREER TITLES FROM TEN SPEED PRESS

Written by a seasoned career journalist, this practical guide helps prospective career changers develop a sound exit strategy or take stock after a layoff, prepare for economic and emotional challenges during the transition, and make strides toward their next work life.

Strategies for Successful Career Change
$16.99 paper (Canada: $21.99)
978-1-58008-824-4

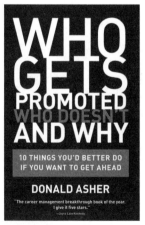

According to career guru Donald Asher, advancement at work is less about skillsets and more about strategy. This book details exactly what puts one employee on the fast track to an exceptional career, while another stays on the treadmill to mediocrity.

Who Gets Promoted, Who Doesn't, and Why
$14.95 paper (Canada: $18.95)
978-1-58008-820-6

TEN SPEED PRESS
Berkeley

MORE BUSINESS CLASSICS
FROM TEN SPEED PRESS

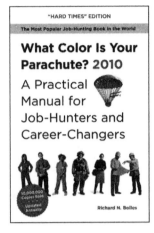

The number one job-hunting book of all time, this complete guide helps first-time job seekers as well as second and encore career changers. By focusing not only on finding a job, but also on finding a life that has meaning and purpose, *Parachute* is the most comprehensive career guide around.

What Color Is Your Parachute?
(revised annually)
$18.99 paper (Canada: $23.99)
978-1-58008-987-6

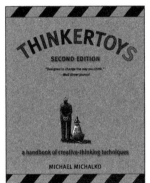

This handbook of creative thinking techniques offers ingenious strategies for approching problems in unconventional ways. Fun and thought-provoking exercises demonstrate how to create original ideas that can improve the way you work.

Thinkertoys
$19.95 paper (Canada: $24.95)
978-1-58008-773-5

TEN SPEED PRESS
Berkeley

Available from Ten Speed Press wherever books are sold.
www.crownpublishing.com | www.tenspeed.com